Contents

Introduction

GET THE TORIES OUT!

OUR SOCIALIST MEDIA CAMPAIGN

EDITED BY ANDREW GODSELL

Independently Published in Britain 2020

The pieces in this book represent the individual view of each author. The book is published as part of the debate about the way forward for the Labour Party, as we tackle the Tories, drawn from views expressed on social media. The book is not endorsed by the Labour Party, and does not seek to represent the party's official position.

The book is illustrated with memes circulated on Twitter, some of which have been produced by contributors to this book.

If anybody thinks there has been an inadvertent infringement of copyright, please contact the editor, who will deal with this in the next edition. The editor can be found on Twitter @AndrewGodsell.

ISBN 9798617341746

Introduction

When the results of the 2019 General Election were announced, the Conservatives won a majority of 80 seats. Labour were reduced to 202 MPs, the party's smallest total since 1935. This was largely due to the loss of support in areas that voted to leave the European Union – with people disaffected by Labour's switch to the second referendum policy.

The 1935 election had taken place 84 years earlier, when the age at which people were enfranchised was 21. This meant the youngest voters in 1935 were born in 1914. The scale of Labour's defeat in 2019 is unparalleled in our lifetimes. Or is it? The significantly low level of seats masked the fact that Labour won 10,265,912 votes at the latest election, two and a half years on from 12,878,460 people voting for a radical programme, shaped by Jeremy Corbyn and our mass membership, during 2017.

The 2019 Labour vote total was higher than we received in three other elections in the current century – 2005 (Labour majority), 2010 (hung Parliament led to Con-Dem coalition), and 2015 (Tory Election Fraud proved to be the reason for their win). Labour's vote in 2017 had been exceeded in only four previous General Elections, those of 1950, 1951 (a defeat despite winning a higher popular vote than the Tories), 1966, and 1997.

The 2017 Election brought an increase in the Labour vote compared to the previous such contest of 3,531,187. This was the second largest gain of votes in Labour's history. The biggest leap occurred in 1945, when Labour won power with 3,982,758 more votes than in the preceding election. With elections on hold during World War Two, the poll prior to 1945 had been held a whole decade earlier, taking us back to the 1935 result.

These figures suggest that talk of an existential crisis for the Labour Party at the end of 2019, and into 2020, is premature. Without the concern from 2016 leave voters that Labour was abandoning them, combined with the massive mainstream media attack on us, we could have repeated our historically high vote of 2017. That vote had removed the small Tory majority in the House of Commons, when Theresa May, and her numerous Blue Tick supporters with Ipads (who masqueraded as journalists), thought she was on course to increase it.

The current crisis for Labour is largely a false construct from the opponents of our party. Sadly this narrative is being amplified by the misnamed "moderates" in Labour. Their zealous nostalgia for Blairite Neoliberalism attacked the resurgent left during 2016, with the "Chicken Coup" and "Labour Purge", notorious failed attempts to break Corbyn and his supporters.

In the months since our 2019 Election defeat, I have seen an enormous amount of positive activity on Twitter. There have been inspirational ideas about rebuilding support for the Labour Party and Socialism. Many of us strongly believe the Tories will fail to deliver on empty pledges they made to win the Election. The Conservative Party have little or no interest in the working people who lent them votes to "Get Brexit Done". Months before Boris Johnson came up with his slogan, we were saying "Get The Tories Out". Actually we were often using #GTTO, one of the popular hashtags introduced by Rachael Swindon, a woman who has been a massive influence in putting the Socialist message into British social media.

The strong advocacy of continued radical Socialism in the Labour Party, as the best way to challenge and defeat the Tories, gave me an idea. I suggested, in January 2020, that we should capture some of this excellent content, in a cheap paperback, to spread our message beyond Twitter.

The response was very encouraging. Within a few hours, several people offered to contribute to the book. In the next few days, excellent pieces were sent to me. I put a summary of the developing plan on my Blog, and pointed people towards this with a Twitter thread. Over the course of a few weeks, more pieces arrived. Meanwhile exchanges with the growing group of writers, via Twitter and email, produced new ideas for content, including some great memes to illustrate the book.

Little more than a month on from the original idea, the book was published! This rapid arrival enabled the book to be part of a debate on the future of our party, during the Labour leadership election then in progress. The plan was to produce an expanded, and updated, book after the leadership contest concluded, and here it is.

Many thanks are due to all of the authors, who quickly saw the positive possibilities of this project. The pieces that follow each speak for themselves. They express the experience and views of individual campaigners, who are working with others – both online and in the real world – to build the collective strength of our movement.

Thank you for reading. Hopefully you will be enthused to share our message on social media, and show people this book!

Andrew Godsell

June 7 2020

Alone We May be Small, But Together We Are Mighty

Kimberley @LeftWingKim

Labour Party member
Keep an open mind, but not so open your brains fall out!
You don't need a weapon, you were born one.

Joined Twitter 2010
3,600 Followers

This is from my application to join the Labour Party in 2019. It might help some people remember why they joined, when we are struggling with the current political situation.

In years to come, I want to be able to look my new-born son in the eye and tell him that I did my part. I didn't stand by and do nothing as our country ripped itself to shreds. I stood up and voted for the side that would take climate change seriously, that would eliminate the need for food banks and give the homeless a safe place to sleep.

I want him to know I did not stand by and watch as our country was corrupted even further by a Prime Minister who thinks it's acceptable to lie and use racist remarks.

Our country will be damaged beyond repair if we see another 5 years of Conservative rule. Whatever it takes, we must reunite our country and repair the damage austerity has brought upon us.

I want to set an example to my son so he will forever know that alone we may be small, but together we are mighty.

The time for change is now. For the many, not the few.

Never Trust a Tory

Bob Miller @hctbn

Ageing lefty electronic CEng with a missus & 2 kids. I like steak (blue), music, BBC R4 extra, F1, and driving my Land Rover (so global warming is my fault!)

Joined Twitter 2011
1,300 Followers

Wrote this Twitter thread in anger, starting at 01:22 on Friday December 13 2019, General Election night. On reflection I can say that I stick by every word of it. Until we get MSM journos with the balls to hold power to account, Bar Stewards like Bozo will be able to do whatever they want.

You voted Tory?

What the fuck were

you thinking?

If the exit polls are correct this is not a victory for Bozo.

It is a victory for the cynics running the Tory campaign who correctly analysed that the Tory front bench are unelectable and kept the British public from seeing them (although there's been enough evidence over the last 9 years).

It's been a victory for the billionaires that own and run the majority of the British press.

It's been a victory for the BBC that has cheer led the Tory party from beginning to end.

It's a victory for every pathetic journo that has failed to hold power to account and considers that attacking the opposition that has no control of what the government does is more important than attacking the government.

That government has deliberately implemented a raft of policies that have asset stripped the country to give everything to their billionaire mates.

That has forced millions into poverty.

That has killed homeless people on a daily basis.

That has wrecked the NHS and thrown away 70 years of excellence for their 40 pieces of silver.

That has wrecked the economy and increased national debt from £780 billion to £1,700 billion.

That has implemented benefits policies that have resulted in the deaths of many that they have declared "fit for work".

That has wrecked our standing in the world.

That has allowed poor people to be housed in buildings that are quite literally death traps and even knowing that done nothing about it.

That has actively implemented a racist and discriminatory hostile environment.

That has deliberately and consistently lied to cover up its failings and cover up what it is really doing.

That has reduced police numbers and watched knife crime go through the roof.

They have blamed it all on Labour who have been out of power for the last 9 years.

I hold journalism just as responsible for this whole mess as I do all the bastards in the government, that sees the country simply as a source of resources to be stripped and given away and fuck the poor.

Talk to People, Listen and Help Them

Wolfie @tpopularfront

Consultant to @LeftPhoenix
"Notorious, dangerous, unofficial Labour Propaganda Machine"
Pro Corbyn, Pro Palestine. Anti-Tory

Joined Twitter 2017
26,800 Followers

A Twitter Thread posted on December 14 2019 – the day after we learned of Labour's General Election defeat.

My thoughts on where we need to go.

We need to have an election-style canvass in every constituency at least once a year. A quick questionnaire to ascertain people's concerns and where they think Labour have gone wrong. Feed it back into a database.

We need to select our candidates for the next election now. Preferably local people, who can get into their constituencies, listen to people, put pressure on the Tory incumbent, and sow seeds for the next election. We need to regain trust.

As well as looking where we've failed, we should look at where we've done well. Look to Liverpool, and see why working people are so engaged with Labour. Is it the opposition to the media, strong grassroots, engagement through football?

More than anything we have to counter the media. They are never going to be on our side. We get into communities, do voluntary work without being overly political, but join with charities and movements. We have to understand what is going on in each constituency.

The next five years are going to be hard for most people, but especially hard for the people we lost. We have the numbers, the Tories have the media. We have to use our strengths and talk to people, listen and help them. Isn't that what Socialism is about?

How did Labour Lose its "Red Wall" Towns?

Wayne Rhodes @Sheff_socialist

Working class lad from South Yorks.
Socialist and proud of it.
Still waiting for that great leap forwards.

Blog: sheffsocialist.wordpress.com

Joined Twitter 2014
1,900 Followers

A long Twitter Thread posted at the end of 2019, and then Blogged in early 2020

I come from a genuine working class family.

Grandparents were miners and domestic cleaning staff.

Dad was a butcher, mum was a cleaner and when she remarried after their divorce she married a miner. I grew up in a two up two down terrace house that my parents rented from the local Co-op society and then moved into a council house on the Kendray council housing estate in Barnsley when my mum remarried.

One grandad was a NUM union rep (at Woolley Colliery alongside Arthur Scargill).

My other grandad was a NUPE union rep.

Mum and her sister were both UNISON reps.

I guess what I'm trying to get across is that we were a proper Labour supporting family, cut us in half and we would have had the word Labour running through us like a stick of Blackpool rock.

And yet in this election I was the only one of my family still voting Labour, despite all of us living in traditional "Red Wall" Labour areas.

I'm in Sheffield but my family is split across the Barnsley area, some in Dan Jarvis' constituency, some in Stephanie Peacock's and some in the Penistone area that's just turned Tory.

So how the hell did this happen???

Why did my parents and close friends and family vote Brexit Party?

Why did my siblings and my aunts and uncles vote Tory?

They can't just be dismissed as stupid or ignorant people. I grew up around them and thought that the values and beliefs I hold dear had all been instilled in me from these self-same people. We all lived through Thatcher's annihilation of our communities when she went after the unions and destroyed Barnsley both after and during the Miners' strike. My step-dad even losing his job when Woolley Colliery was closed and never working meaningfully again.

So how the hell did they all come to abandon Labour and vote for parties whose policies are the complete antithesis of their own needs and aspirations??

To answer that you've got to look further back than just this last few weeks or months or even the last couple of years.

You've got to look a lot further back.

Before the Miners' strike in '84 everyone I knew lived and worked in Barnsley, my grandparents' jobs were in Barnsley, my parents jobs were in Barnsley, my aunts and uncles all worked in Barnsley as it seemed did all my friends' families.

The aftermath of the strike changed all that.

Most people were employed at the coalmines or in industry connected to the coalmines or in the service industries like the shops and pubs etc where the hard working miners and their families spent their wages. When those wages went then so did the local economy.

New Labour in 1997 gave people hope of a change but all they brought to the area were low paid minimum wage jobs to replace high paid skilled industrial jobs. People thought that when New Labour were elected that they would regenerate and revitalise these traditional working class Labour heartlands.

They didn't.

Areas like Barnsley just got left behind, their Labour votes taken for granted.

Life had changed. Only my mum still worked in Barnsley. I moved to Sheffield because of work. My dad ended up in Stoke where he met my step-mum before they returned to Barnsley. My brother, his wife and most other family members worked in other nearby towns and cities, even though they still lived in Barnsley.

Some like my step-dad and aunt and uncle relied on the benefits system to see them through to retirement age.

Then along came the banking crisis, followed by the high street crisis that saw the likes of Woolworths bite the dust. Quickly followed by a Tory and Lib Dem government pushing their disastrous austerity policies. Areas like Barnsley took another hammering.

Jobs again lost in the local economy which had never truly recovered from Thatcher thanks to New Labour's indifference. Cuts to essential council services and cuts to the NHS locally meaning longer waiting lists and crowded doctors' waiting rooms.

And in amongst all this come Nigel Farage and Boris Johnson. This pair of poisonous bastards gave everyone in areas like Barnsley exactly what they needed, exactly what they wanted....

Someone to blame.

Immigrants.

Immigrants let into this country by the EU.

Immigrants taking all our jobs.

Immigrants using our NHS for free.

Immigrants given priority for our council houses.

Immigrants filling up our doctors' waiting rooms.

You see it couldn't just be the Tories' fault that things were rough because it hadn't gotten any better in areas like Barnsley whilst Labour had been in power.

So it had to be someone else's fault.

So Farage and Johnson must be correct when they blame immigrants and tells us all the other politicians don't understand and just don't care.

Narratives that have been pushed relentlessly by Farage, Vote Leave, Johnson and plenty of others over the past few years.

Farage and Johnson must be correct if the news that we see on the telly says the same thing and asks them to come on all the time to talk about it.

Farage and Johnson must be correct if the newspapers all print the same stories blaming immigrants for taking our jobs and our houses and clogging up our NHS.

And Farage and Johnson must be correct if everyone on Facebook is posting the same memes about it especially if fat Brenda from the local chippy is posting it because she obviously knows her stuff!!!!

Under Thatcher we knew who to blame, the Tories.

But under Blair who did we need to blame for life getting no better in places like Barnsley? Yes we had Sure Start, yes we had the Minimum wage regulations, yes we had peace in Northern Ireland and yes we had more funding in the NHS but when we lost the heavy industry and the coalmines that provided most of the jobs and most of the economic wealth we lost our soul, our community and our pride. And we weren't sure who to blame this time, our loyalties to Labour confused us so we started to not care anymore. Politicians were all the same, none of them cared for us, they only cared for themselves.

Then along came Cameron and austerity and who do we blame for that?

Not the politicians because they've told us that we are all in this together and there is no other way, we have to all make sacrifices no matter whether rich or poor, privileged or not. So we blame the immigrants, the ones that the EU are "forcing" us to take. And by default because we tend to class anyone who's different to us as a potential immigrant then we blame any and all ethnic minorities.

All of this whipped up to a frenzy since 2016 by the likes of Farage, Vote Leave, Tommy Robinson, Katie Hopkins, Hartley-Brewer, Newton-Dunn, Rod Liddle, The *Sun*, The *Daily Mail* etc and Boris Johnson and his Tory cohorts.

Aided and abetted by the usual cast of idiots at the BBC, ITV and Sky.

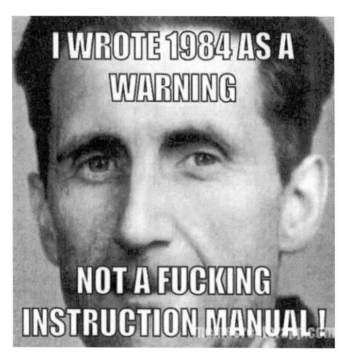

Sadly I watched this unfold with my own family over the last 3-4 years and didn't do anything like enough to try and counter it. I ignored the initial flurry of anti-EU comments and social media posts from them partly because I was voting leave too, albeit for completely different reasons, those being a distrust of the fairness of the CAP and CFP and a distrust of the EU not to resurrect the by then defunct talks around the TTIP trade agreement. Ironic really when you realise that Johnson's election victory leaves us facing a trade deal with the US that resembles TTIP on steroids. I spent far too long just telling them to stop posting racist bollocks when they shared Farage or UKIP memes bemoaning immigration instead of actually sitting down and explaining why the stuff they were reading, watching and sharing was wrong and factually false.

I ignored the anti-Corbyn comments because I just assumed that when it came around to election time they would just hold their noses and vote Labour as they had all done for years previous regardless of the popularity of whichever figure head was leading the party at that particular moment in time, just as they all had in 2017.

I finally realised I hadn't done enough when the election campaign kicked in.

I only work part time now and that's from home so I'd decided to get fully involved in the campaign both on the ground canvassing locally and by way of posting lots of Labour manifesto info on social media. Boy did I get the shock of my life when I started posting stuff about Labour's manifesto plans on Facebook.

I got absolutely frigging mullered...........

By my own family members and close friends.

My posts were full of comments from them with arguments and rhetoric that had been drummed into them by Farage, Cummings and Johnson over the last few years. My timeline was full of anti-Labour memes. It got that bad that I ended up deleting my Facebook account. I ended the year with myself and a lot of my close friends and even some family members no longer on speaking terms.

Then you realise it's not just yourself and your own family that's experiencing this.

You speak to a friend in Rotherham and find they've had the exact same experiences. You get a call from your son in the armed forces to tell you that he's up on a charge for getting into a scuffle with some of his colleagues after being called a Muslim-loving terrorist supporting traitor just for sharing some Labour stuff himself on social media.

Living in Sheffield possibly led to me being a little isolated from Labour's problems. It's a multi-cultural city and apart from the usual quota of knobheads and Tommy Robinson types we all live side by side with few serious problems. Brexit didn't seem to be as big an issue inside the city as it did in the out-laying towns.

But in fairness things never got as desperate or demoralising in the cities as they did in the towns and old industrial areas. We saw quite a lot of regeneration and investment especially in transport links that other places nearby didn't.

We weren't looking quite so hard for someone to blame.

There is no denying that Corbyn had a definite image problem on the doorsteps.

He had a massive target on his back and the mainstream media were able to hit its bull's-eye with alarming regularity and to devastating effect. But this hadn't been insurmountable during the 2017 election, even in areas like Barnsley and Rotherham.

And I genuinely believe that had Jeremy Corbyn been just as intolerant towards immigrants and ethnic minorities as the Tories were he would have picked up enough of those voters who despised him personally to have had a very different result. After all the country happily elected an absolute racist bigot in Johnson instead of Corbyn.

That's an absolutely disgraceful situation to find ourselves in especially when you also come to the realisation that members of your own family, your community and your close friends also voted this way.

How does Labour get voters like these back???

More to the point do we actually want them back???

Do we really want to try to appeal to a group of voters who are far too willing to blame immigration and ethnic minorities for all our ills? And yes we may have had the policies that would have addressed the problems that led to them voting for the Tories / Brexit Party but you can't enact those policies if you don't get elected into government in the first place.

Would a different leader have made a difference to these voters??

Yes, to some of them.

Would a different Brexit policy have made a difference?

Definitely, to most of them.

Did they vote this way because they're racist???

Undoubtedly so for a large number of them but no, not for most them.

I would hope that it isn't a deep seated racism that's to blame here, rather just a reaction to the constant and unrelenting malign influence of the mainstream media, alongside targeted Facebook memes and also persuasive snake oil salesmen like Farage, Johnson and Cummings.

But I guess we won't know that for definite until 2024 when we go to the polls once more, with a different Labour leader, with "getting Brexit done" no longer an issue and with the realisation that even outside of the EU nothing has changed in Barnsley and similar towns under this bastard of a Tory government.

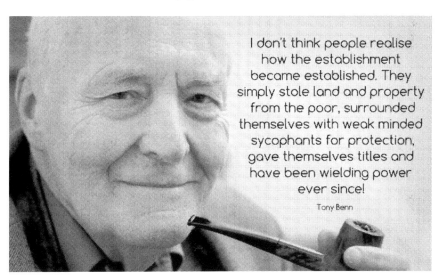

I don't think people realise how the establishment became established. They simply stole land and property from the poor, surrounded themselves with weak minded sycophants for protection, gave themselves titles and have been wielding power ever since!

Tony Benn

How Labour Increased its Vote Share in the Isle of Wight Against the Odds

Julian Critchley @DisIdealist

Disappointed idealist.

Blog: disidealist.wordpress.com

Joined Twitter 2014
5,900 Followers

Reflections from just after the General Election, which were soon re-Blogged by "Left Foot Forward".

This article sets out the experience of the campaign from the perspective of one of the tiny handful of constituencies where Labour increased its vote, this being the Isle of Wight!

We didn't win, of course. That's for next time! But we did increase our vote and our vote share when Labour was losing votes and vote share pretty much everywhere else. We squeezed the votes of the Lib Dems and Greens in an election where the Lib Dems and Greens were not only increasing their votes nationally, but were being recommended as the tactical option locally by every one of those tediously irritating tactical voting sites.

So the result may not have shaken even David Cameron's garden shed to its foundations, and nobody's going to write a book about how the Isle of Wight Labour Party marched triumphantly from second place to, er, a slightly better second place. But this was an accomplishment which very seriously bucked the national trend nevertheless.

I don't think the Labour Party, as it currently tears at its own entrails in grief, should leave any stones unturned in seeing how it might go about the next election better. And just off the south coast of North Island, the Isle of Wight is a particularly large and lovely stone to examine.

Firstly, I'll set out what we felt were the main factors for our relatively successful campaign. I don't think anyone will find these things particularly original or shocking. It's just the basics of good campaigning.

Secondly, a little sting in the tail, because I'll make some comparisons with campaigns in our top defensive and target seats, and those comparisons aren't great. The party's factional war has moved to a new battleground over whether the loss was the fault of the Right for forcing a change in Brexit policy, or the Left for installing Corbyn.

Yet there's a "forgotten front" which is being neglected, which is that in some places, our campaigning appears to have been just not good enough.

Context – the Isle of Wight

The Isle of Wight is the largest constituency in the country. It also happens to be considerably whiter, older and Brexitier (62% Leave) than most places.

We have no higher education institution, so few students. We're short on public sector professionals and urban liberals, and any minority group you care to mention is more of a minority here than in most of the country.

We've also never had a Labour MP, or a Labour council. At present, we have no Labour councillors at all. In short, according to the various pollsters and their cunning "tribes" of voters, we're the least promising territory for Labour you can imagine.

Yet in 2017, we doubled our vote, moving from fourth (yes, fourth) place behind Tories, UKIP and the Greens, to second place. This despite a ferocious tactical voting campaign by the Greens in which they outspent us by 100%, and which was supported by some of our own people on and off the island.

In the 2019 election, we raised our vote further, again in the face of unanimous recommendations from tactical voting sites for the Greens, in whose favour the Lib Dems had stood down their candidate. And of course we did so in the context of a national electoral disaster which saw Labour's vote drop 8%, and rather more in constituencies with similar demographics to ours.

By demographics, we probably have to correct a misconception here. The Isle of Wight is not a wealthy place. It certainly has wealthy people, particularly older retirees. But we're actually quite similar to plenty of traditionally Labour seats. We are, in short, exactly the sort of place where the Labour vote dropped by a large amount on December 12. Yet we increased our vote and our vote share.

Brexit buggered us, as thousands of our 2017 Labour Leave voters left us. So that small increase masked our attracting a rather larger number of replacement voters.

I know that we're all scheduled to be in the meeting marked "bitter factional warfare" for the next few months, but perhaps we shouldn't lose sight of the fact that not everything that happened in every constituency was beyond the ability of the local team to influence at least a little.

Now, to misquote Montell Jordan, this is how we did it.

Start the campaign early

We started our campaign for the 2019 election in June 2017. It was clear then that this was not a government which could last a full term, and many were predicting another election in months, not years. So while we certainly didn't keep going at full campaign pace, we never fully took our foot off the gas.

Throughout the period we aimed to release one press notice every week, preferably about local issues, to get us coverage in the local media. When there are no local stories, there's always a local angle you can try to national stories.

Demanding answers from the current Tory MP about why he voted this way was always a good way of ensuring that local voters knew that the Labour Party was holding him to account. Any local story about council or national cuts would also inevitably see a quote from Labour popping into every local editor's inbox.

In addition, we aimed for an update to the party's main shop window, our public Facebook page, every other day. By 2019, that was an update every day. This was very important because it built a page following which was going to be absolutely central to the 2019 campaign. We'll return to this.

Not all the press notices were picked up. Not all the social media posts gathered lots of attention. There were fallow periods. But by the time this election was called, we had been making the biggest non-Tory noise locally for over two years. A good way of measuring our impact was the complaints from below-the-line Tories on local media about the local Labour Party getting too much coverage.

Get a good candidate

We had an excellent candidate. One of the advantages of being a below-the-radar seat is that we don't attract ambitious careerists who can only find us on a map because of the clue in the name. Nor does party HQ ever consider imposing anyone. We get to choose freely.

After my run as accidental candidate in 2017, I decided at the last minute I didn't want to do it again. This was fortunate for us, because it opened the door to Richard Quigley, a local small businessman with manic energy and no background (and therefore no baggage or enemies) in local politics.

Crucially, he also brought with him two key attributes. Firstly, he was genuinely committed to the policies of the party, which meant his answers were always authentic and convincing. Secondly, and unlike me, he genuinely appears to like people. I don't understand that, but it certainly worked for us.

I don't want to overegg the importance of the candidate. After all, every political party could draw up a long list of incompetents, crooks, sociopaths and fools who have nevertheless been elected, and a similarly long list of wonderful, worthy, committed saints who haven't got anywhere. But in an election where it often felt like people were looking for reasons not to vote for us, the fact that our candidate persisted in only giving reasons to back us was an enormous help.

Win the real world visibility war

In 2017, I'd often had received the comment "I didn't know Labour was active on the island". We needed people to see us as not just a viable party, but the biggest. Simultaneously, we knew early on that we would be fighting something which I know other CLPs experienced: shame.

The "othering" of Corbyn had long extended past him alone to encompass the entire party. To support Corbyn's Labour was, according to most of our national media, somehow beyond common decency. We knew this had happened before the campaign started, and one of our earliest priorities was to create a safe space for supporters.

Not many people are brave enough to put their heads above the parapet when bullets are flying, if they're on their own. But give them a few visible comrades willing to go over the top alongside them, and that can change. Signage was the offline half of the battle to create a psychological safe space for potential Labour supporters to feel that they weren't alone, and there was a point in their support and their vote.

We prioritised the ordering of signs, boards and posters, and set up an efficient manufacture and distribution method. Then we emailed all 850+ members every other day throughout the campaign with a central contact point for signage. We would almost always get signs to requests within 24 hours. We also specifically targeted the (very expensive) garden signs on the streets with high traffic. Cul-de-sacs in the middle of the countryside got a window poster. The last sign was put up late on December 11 in a street which was used to go to a polling station. In total, we put out 240 garden signs and 750 A3 window posters.

We also printed 30,000 leaflets with local printers, in addition to the 76,000 freepost leaflets which slowly – oh so very, very slowly – were printed by the national party. The leaflets had a mini poster on the reverse, so we were also effectively giving out 30,000 more window posters for cars and homes.

None of this is rocket science, but it's a vital building block. There was unprecedented intimidation, abuse (and destruction of signage) in this election. We needed to show our potential supporters that we were out there with them in force.

Maximise activist efficiency

This was an early decision to repeat what we didn't do in 2017. We didn't canvass.

It's a case of maths. Every CLP will know that the ratio of members to activists is not great. Our 850 members yields about 100 who will attend meetings, 50 who'll deliver leaflets and help out, and 30 who are confident and comfortable talking to voters face to face. Of those 30, all will hand a leaflet out in a town centre, but only a dozen or so are really up for the intensely intimidating business of knocking on a stranger's door in the dark and asking them to vote Labour.

I've done it. I hate it, but I'm quite good at it. When excluding houses with no answer, and those who say "no thanks" immediately, I reckon I end up having about 8-10 actual conversations in an hour at my very best, and 75% of them will be already committed voters for us or someone else. So maybe 2 or 3 actual undecideds an hour. If all 12 of our willing canvassers were able to turn up at the same time, we'd maybe get 20-30 undecided conversations in an hour. We have an electorate of 113,021, living in an entire county of 76,000 houses in over a hundred different towns and villages spread out over 148 square miles.

So we didn't canvass.

But we still needed to have those conversations and, above all, win the visibility war. So while our opponents were trudging a fraction of the island's streets, unseen, we were in the town centres.

Without the in-your-face intensity of doorstep canvassing, we had more bodies willing to stand in town centres, hand out leaflets and engage in conversation. On each weekend, we had people out in most or all of the six major population centres on the Island, very visibly wearing red and handing out our leaflets. We were seen by thousands more people than we could have reached canvassing, in more places.

The cherry on the top of the visibility cake was the "March For Labour". Fifty activists were involved in an event where most walked the 7 miles between the two main towns of Ryde and Newport. All decked out in red, carrying banners, this wasn't an attempt to pay homage to Mao's Long March. It was done because it took us along the busiest road on the island, where we were seen by many hundreds of cars over a four hour stretch, as well as many hundreds more people in both Ryde and Newport.

And it was an odd enough event that those people spoke to other people about seeing these red-clad nutters marching down the road getting beeped by passing cars. As well as demonstrating commitment, it showed numbers and strength – no other party could put something like that on. It was unusual enough to allow us coverage in the local media, but more on that later.

There are rituals in elections – doorstep canvassing is one, standing outside a polling booth with a clipboard is another. These can make sense if you're in a tight marginal and have the numbers of activists to not only find out where your vote is, but to get bodies round to encourage it out on the day. Few constituencies have that capacity, yet many which don't probably still perform the rituals. It's a good idea to review those actions to see whether more bangs for the activist buck can be had elsewhere.

Go to the people, don't make them come to you

The local Green Party hired a shop in Newport for the campaign. It must have cost them a packet. We took our candidate to the pub.

Lots of pubs.

We knew we couldn't wait for people to come to us, we had to go and find them. So we organised multiple meet-the-candidate events, which we promoted, in pubs. The pubs liked it, because of the cash behind the bar. The local members liked it, because they could chat to the candidate (and drink). And we got noticed by, and spoke to, people who would never have dreamed of walking into a political party's shop.

We weren't packing them out like a Corbyn rally, but it was another way of being visible, or providing a safe space, and of accessing real-life networks of people who used the pubs. Even if they didn't talk to us, they saw us, and they talked about it to their mates. Word got around. Labour were out and about, and down the pub.

The candidate also visited care homes and cafes, specifically to meet and listen to (note listen to, not talk at) important local subsets like care workers and small business people. Even where there might only be half a dozen attendees, we would then see one or more of them in a neutral online space saying "I met that Labour guy, and he was really nice…". There's a multiplier effect from each event. We kept the candidate busy.

Fight for local media

Slightly bizarrely, our local media was less willing to cover press releases from us during the campaign than it was before the election was called. We were told by one editor of a local online news source that press releases during the election were "just campaigning, not news".

It rapidly became clear that the local media didn't see it as their job to communicate policies to the voters. Our original plan to issue a press notice from the candidate every day linked to the daily campaign briefing from HQ was quickly abandoned after the first 7 or 8 were universally ignored.

But the local media still had a role to play. It reached parts of the electorate which we couldn't reach directly online, particularly the more elderly section of the population who read the print versions. And not just the two county newspapers, but the monthly periodical which is delivered to every house on the island. We quickly bought and arranged advert space in all of them. Adverts are no substitute for coverage, so we had to manufacture some.

I'd love to tell you we were cunning enough to plan it all, but mostly it was about being fleet-footed and seizing opportunities. The Tories did us a favour by writing a public letter to us asking us about Brexit which the media covered, along with our reply.

Clearly it was designed to promote their central campaign message, but sauce for the goose etc, so we returned the favour with a letter about the NHS. These letter exchanges, though ritual, not only allowed us to promote our key message, but also reinforced the message that this was a red-blue election, causing real harm to the tactical voting campaign of the Greens.

Various other opportunities presented themselves. Tory loon Suella Braverman announced on TV that there was going to be a new hospital on the Isle of Wight (there isn't). Our own Tory, Bob Seely, announced Labour planned to shut down the local Free School (we didn't).

We got a tip-off about a night of chaos in the local A&E. The key was being able to respond very rapidly. In all cases we had press notices out in a couple of hours maximum, and we followed that up with phone calls to the journalists to exert a little persuasion to run the story. We adapted quickly to the stance the local media chose to take, and continued to get coverage.

Win the online War

It's hardly a revelation to say that the online world has become the crucial battleground of 21st Century campaigning. Even on the Isle of Wight, where we only recently stopped believing electricity was witchcraft. We knew that this was where we had the best chance of getting our message across to a largely disengaged electorate, untainted by media bias. It became even more vital when the local media chose to abdicate the role of communicating policies.

Targeted local material

Fortunately, we were ready. I mentioned earlier that we had been preparing since 2017. We had focused on Facebook. It has greater reach into the non-politically-committed electorate than other social media, and it's the most important platform for the age profile of the Island.

From the end of 2017, we maintained our public Facebook page as a shopfront for the local party. It was not a free-for-all forum filled with interminable trollish arguments, or a CLP noticeboard of no interest to anyone but the CLP. It was a sales pitch. It needed to be relatively professional and relentlessly positive. It also needed to be updated frequently so that it regularly pushed our news into other accounts, as well as becoming a place which our hundreds of Facebook-using members checked regularly and shared from.

We had observed what "sold" from the Facebook page over the previous two years. Which stories always did well (ferries and the local NHS, since you ask), and which did little trade (national-only issues, and issues which affected relatively small sub-groups of the local population). Video clips and catchy picture memes were shared many times, walls of text weren't. There's nothing radical about these observations, which is why the upcoming comparison might shock a few readers.

So we set out at the start of the election to ensure that there was a distinctive local flavour to as much as possible. Memes badged with the Island Labour logo were produced for national policy announcements, with text on how they'd affect us. Eye-catching shareable digs at the local Tory MP or council were created. And we produced a series of short, snappy videos of our candidate which looked and sounded authentic (because they were – I filmed them on my phone while his dog tried to get in the shot).

The point was that much of the material was seen as locally relevant, because we'd produced it, twisted it to local issues, and branded it locally. This was a very specific conversation which Island Labour was having with Island voters, in the midst of a national election.

Use your people's networks

Of course, no amount of excellent material is of any use if people don't see it. So we encouraged our online membership daily to share material from the main page. If each individual member has 200 Facebook friends, you only need 20 of them to share your meme, and you've just reached a potential 4000 voters. Then some of them share it further, and so on.

Some statistics give you an idea of the impact. Over the four weeks of the election, we reached more than 118,000 people. More than 72,000 "engaged" with one or more of our posts, meaning they reacted to it, clicked on the link, shared or commented. 9 of our posts reached more than 20,000 people each. 32 posts reached more than 4,000 people. Even allowing for duplication, these are big numbers, reaching places in our electorate which nothing else could get to.

One way we knew we were reaching the parts of the electorate we didn't normally reach was the huge spike in abusive messages from Brexit Party and Tory supporters. They were seeing our material repeatedly, because it was being shared into their Facebook feeds either directly or indirectly. Although I won't claim it was pleasant wiping the virtual right-wing spittle from our comments page twice daily, I was conscious that every illiterate troll whose comment was hidden meant we were reaching more local voters.

This was just the direct social media. We produced a section called "helpful memes", which allowed our members and other sympathetic users to copy the pictures and paste them on elsewhere. During the campaign, I saw numerous memes which originated with us being shared in the "neutral" social media community pages around the island. These wouldn't count on our direct statistics, but were still part of our online marketing, and a very effective part. Posts on neutral ground from people who weren't well-known local Labour figures had greater value because of their perceived authenticity in peer-to-peer networks.

So, back to the stats, which I watched like a trainspotter with OCD for the duration. The first two weeks of the campaign, we pushed from our usual weekly c5,000 engagement numbers up to 20,000 per week, and then carried on going. For the last two weeks of the campaign, we averaged over 20,000, and the final week was 28,400 engagements (likes, comments and shares).

Our Green opponents, competing with us to reach the Remain voters in the constituency, were always far below us, spending much of the last two weeks at 25-33% of our engagements, while the Tories only learned how to play with Facebook in the final week, and managed to creep up to 9,000 by the end. Our main rival was actually Stephen Morgan's excellent online campaign just over the water in Portsmouth South. We had clearly surpassed him by the last week, right up until the final day when – through some dastardly magic – he suddenly rocketed past us (the swine).

Why am I telling you this? Well here's some information which will make grim reading for Labour supporters.

On election day, before the result, I visited the Facebook sites of CLPs in our main English defensive and offensive marginal seats, and used Facebook's comparison "Insight" tool to look at their levels of engagement.

I am proud of our efforts, but I was astonished to find that our small band of amateurs – in a historically safe Tory seat, with no paid staff, and no assistance from the regional or national party – should have been running a bigger Facebook campaign than all but two of our top target seats, and all but two of our most vulnerable defensive seats. In some instances, our online engagement was literally more than twenty times the size of that in seats which had tiny majorities.

I didn't understand how this could be the case, and so I went and looked at these pages to get a qualitative feel for what the quantitative data was telling me. In too many cases, the picture was grim. No memes, no positivity, no clips. Nothing that would entice people to share and spread the message. In several cases there weren't even any policies.

What I saw far too much of, was a simple picture of the candidate standing with the same half dozen people on a different dark, cold street, holding leaflets and trying to look as if they wouldn't rather be anywhere else. Occasionally, there'd be a picture of the candidate next to a celebrity politician (David Miliband seemed to get around a few of these places), or even just a celebrity (and so did Ross Kemp). But the statistics were terrible. Nobody was sharing it. Nobody cared. Nobody knew.

I was also struck by how many times I was seeing the same handful of people in those endless pictures of leafleting. Meanwhile, I was aware that we had involved dozens and dozens of enthusiastic activists in our various activities. The contrast was stark.

I scrolled as far back as November 21 on one candidate's Facebook page, covering the last 3 weeks of the campaign, and found not one single post about any Labour policy in this election. Not one. Just pictures of the candidate and the same handful of leafleters, plus a couple of the candidate and a couple of grandees. Their engagement rate was less than 10% of ours. In a heartland seat with an immense Labour tradition. This pattern repeated itself in others.

It may well be that the seats in question had absolutely superb offline campaigns. But that's not an excuse for missing this battleground. Online campaigning is absolutely vital, particularly on Facebook. In some of our most marginal seats, we were essentially doing very little of it.

Local campaigns matter

This is conjecture, but I'll put it out there anyway as a contribution to the debate raging about this election. We in the Island were able to run the campaign we did because we have, by and large, embraced and encouraged the new and enthusiastic post-2015 members. Our Corbyn-sceptics stayed on board, and while they may not have been the most active local members, they did their bit, to their enormous credit.

That energy and genuine enthusiasm meant people gave up their time and skills freely to help. It also meant that our candidate, and the core campaign team, were all unashamed and enthusiastic about sharing the policies and promoting the party.

The picture I saw online in several "heartland" marginals gave a very different impression: of candidates who couldn't bring themselves to promote their own party's policies; of hollowed out CLPs with only a handful of members left who are enthusiastic or daft enough to repeatedly go and stuff letterboxes for the candidate; of a sales team who had no faith in what they were selling.

I don't think one has to be a marketing executive to know that it's hard to sell a product when your shop window is empty, you've got no salespeople, and your pitch is telling your intended customer that they shouldn't buy what you've got.

Any visiting alien looking online would have assumed that the Isle of Wight was the Labour heartland, not the "Red Wall". There are questions to be answered by some CLPs, as well as regional and national office in terms of the support they offered the marginals.

Those seats may not have been won anyway, but I can certainly say that it seems more could have been done to try, at least online. In some cases, I would suggest that those seats' fate was sealed even before the campaign: too few bodies, too little groundwork since 2017, not enough energy.

As a final note, I looked at Sedgefield, despite not being one of the top marginals, because an awful lot of press coverage has been given to the fall of Tony Blair's old seat. Maybe its loss was inevitable.

However, the online campaign there managed to engage less than 20% the number of people we reached on the Isle of Wight. There are now more Labour voters on the Isle of Wight than there are in Sedgefield – now that's a quote which should have a few Labour legends spinning in their graves. We worked very hard to win every single one, and we increased our vote.

Just because we could, doesn't of course mean that everyone could, of course. We had a decent-sized Lib Dem / Green vote to squeeze from 2017. We were the insurgent, not the target, which allows for an aggressive, rather than defensive campaign. There was little pressure on us beyond the pressure we placed on ourselves. And the Isle of Wight is lovely, even in the Winter, so it's always a pleasure to be out and about (this advert was brought to you by Visit Isle of Wight). On the flip side, we had no paid staff, no external assistance, little history, and fewer of the demographic groups which are providing the new bedrock of Labour support.

I don't think we did anything startlingly original. Other places also did some or all of the same things. However I'm struck by the way both sides of the Solent, in Portsmouth South and on the Island, bucked the national trend by running similarly energetic online and offline campaigns.

There are many lessons Labour needs to learn before the next election. One of them may well be that we have to fight *every* constituency as hard as Portsmouth South MP Stephen Morgan did, or as we did, or "safe" seats can quickly become rather less safe than we might have thought.

What's Wrong with the S Word?

Rick Evans @Skybluerick1

Dad, Socialist, Autism Awareness, Coventry City fan and Gardener.

Blog: changewemustobservationsfromtheleft.home.blog

Joined Twitter 2012
12,400 Followers

An update of a piece I wrote in 2016, when it was featured by Chelley Ryan on her "Turning the Tide" Blog.

All our enemies have made the 2017 and 2019 General Election defeats about Jeremy Corbyn. The Tories said he was this that or the other, dangerous and unfit to be Prime Minister. He was smeared probably worse than any other politician that I can remember. Except for one who was never leader of the Labour Party, Tony Benn. I can still remember being incandescent with anger reading an article about Benn in the *Sun* in the 1980s. "Benn on the Couch" it was called, the implication being that Tony was mad. You see Benn and Corbyn were smeared and lied about because of what they stand for. While it's true to say the Labour Party has always had the right wing press against them Benn and now Corbyn have had a special kind of hate directed at them.

Corbyn got elected twice as leader. Some thought he was some sort of cult of personality, but some in the party didn't seem to get it wasn't really about Jeremy. It's about the much bigger picture because it's about his beliefs. He has a positive vision, the politics of hope. As Jeremy himself once said "I think it's called Socialism".

There I've said it – the dreaded S word. In the last 25-30 years the S word has become like a swear word and only now because of the rise of Corbyn has it started to get used slightly more. If you were in the Labour Party in the Blair era you weren't supposed to mention it. To some it was like a portal to a nightmare world, long gone. To say it was like admitting you were a dinosaur. You were either patted on the head and told you will think differently when you are older. Or alternatively you would be told "oh yes I agree with a lot of that, but of course it can never happen", based on that age old assumption that somehow humans can't cooperate together because the world is purely dog eat dog.

Except humans are capable of lots of different things – from great love to intense hate, from amazing generosity to enormous greed and all things in between. Everybody has good and bad in them. We can be complicated creatures. But does that mean we can't have a different type of society? That we are forever to live with the politics of the last 30-40 years? That greed is good, the markets are wonderful and somehow the wealth will trickle down from the top to the bottom? Well to me and increasing numbers of people, the evidence suggests something different. In that time Britain has become more unequal. Simply put, the rich have got richer and the poor poorer. Deliberately so. Just think about that. Is that progress? How have we fallen for it?

However things are always changing; nothing can stand still. When Jeremy Corbyn won the Labour leadership twice – it was a reaction against the last 30 years. Things have gone too far and now people wanted change. Where there is a cause there will be an effect.

So back to that S word; Socialism. What is it? It probably means different things to different people. At its most basic level it means a more equal, more fair society to live in. Nothing extreme or dangerous about that is there? But I would argue it's more than that. It's about how you can achieve these aims.

On the back of our Labour Party Membership card it says, "for all of us a community in which power, wealth and opportunity are in the hands of the many, not the few". To me Socialism is about redistributing wealth. It's about getting the best healthcare whatever your income, it's about getting the best education whatever your income, it's about giving more say to ordinary people, it's about running public services for the good of communities not private shareholders, it's about giving workers more power in the workplace and indeed in how workplaces are run, it's about a fairer progressive tax system, it's about getting a fair day's pay at work, it's about looking after our planet and having a long term plan instead of looking at a short term profit motive as the number one priority, it's about putting people first. Most of all it's about looking after each other in our society.

Those are some of my ideas of what Socialism is. Does it sound extreme or unattainable? Not to me. Of course the problem has been that for the last 30-40 years the whole agenda, and so debate, has been successfully shifted rightwards. We have constantly been told there is no alternative, we can't afford another way. I would argue now that we can't afford to carry on in the same direction that we need to change course. There are always alternatives but the establishment have never wanted ordinary people to know about them. This of course is why Jeremy Corbyn was attacked so much. The establishment knew that Jeremy was a threat to the status quo and why the severity of attacks on him were on another level. In 2015 when he first put his name forward it was often said he was one of the nicest people in politics. You wouldn't have known that when he won the leadership and had to endure over 4 years of vicious unfounded attacks on his character. The attacks were absolute relentless on him because he is a Socialist.

So I think it's time we reclaimed the word Socialism. It's not something from the past but it's as relevant and needed now more than ever. The demonisation has gone on for far too long. It's time to say it with pride again. To shout it from the roof tops, to say this is what we believe in and we are going to try to make it happen. I am proud to be a Socialist. The world has changed immensely over the last 100 years, but good ideas don't go, they don't die – they live on. Some people say we aren't a Socialist Country – it will never catch on. But let's remember the most Socialist thing a Labour Government has ever done was create the NHS which has also been the most popular. Socialism can be popular. Labour can win with a Socialist Manifesto. But of course no one is pretending that will be easy.

So the million dollar question is how do we do it? How do we get elected a genuine Socialist Labour Government? There's no easy answer to that and as we've seen to say it's a challenge is under playing it. Of course in the last election we had the issue of Brexit too which complicated things tremendously. I believe our Brexit position contributed to our defeat. We tried to make it not the Brexit Election but the Tories successfully made the most of it with their "Get Brexit Done" mantra. But I don't believe our policies were unpopular at all rather it was Brexit and our position on it which torpedoed us. So from that angle our last two manifestos are a fantastic platform to build on and I believe it's vital there's no watering down or rightward drift in policy. This isn't a time to waver and capitulate but to stand firm in our vision and beliefs.

People were attracted to Corbyn because of his hopeful message – that things can change for the better for everyone and that's a message we need to push more. Some had never actually heard this before. When I was a child growing up in the 1970s and early 1980s I remember being told that things are a bit better for every generation. That way progress is made. Our children would be better off than us. At school, in a geography lesson, I remember being taught that in the future people would be working less hours. Well in the last 30-35 years this has not only not happened, but has gone into reverse. The hope has slowly gone. But why should we accept this? Our children deserve better than we had, not less.

Every trick in the book was used to discredit Corbyn by the media. But they very rarely mentioned Socialism only that Labour's plans were pie in the sky or barmy in some way and of course unaffordable. They spent far more time attacking the character of Jeremy Corbyn because they knew that was the easiest way to attack Labour. Society has grown more polarised, more unfair but that doesn't mean we have the wrong vision. A lot of people think things will never change. Our role is to convince them it can and must. That what we say is not only achievable but absolutely vital for the future. No easy task but we cannot carry on for the next 30 years like we have the last, with more disasters for ordinary people while the fat cats get fatter.

Thatcher thought she had destroyed Socialism as a credible idea in this country, that is why she said her greatest success was Tony Blair. She said there was no such thing as society. But there is another way to run society and that's Democratic Socialism. So when someone tells you it will never happen just smile and say yes it will – it has to.

But only when enough people demand it.

Even as a Child I Was a Socialist

Annie Walker @Thunderoad75

#Vegan Corbyn supporter.
Will fight against injustice & cruelty til the end of days.
Love London.
Always & forever Bruce and E St Band. Greatest band in world.

Joined Twitter 2011
2,500 Followers

A friend asked how does my campaigning for animal rights link with my Labour politics? Here is a short outline of a long story! I dedicate this piece to an amazing woman and friend, Apsana Begum MP.

Around five years ago I travelled back home from a local Labour Party meeting, on the bus, with a young woman who really impressed me because of her views and commitment to Socialist values in the Party. She gave me insights into issues surrounding the BAME community and many local concerns and projects of which I was unaware.

She quickly became a friend, and once I said to her "you could be our Prime Minister one day"...she just laughed.

But my story starts years before this...

Even as a child I was a Socialist.

Of course I didn't know what that meant when I was small, but I was always the one who worried if a child at school seemed not to have enough to eat, or was in scruffy clothes, or was left out of games, or bullied by others.

I also loved animals, and was always bringing home injured birds, stray cats and dogs, and crying at films where animals were hurt. After more than 60 years I still haven't seen *Bambi* all the way through after being carried out of the cinema screaming when his mother was killed.

We lived on a council estate in High Barnet, a heartland of so-called Conservative values. The Tory cabinet minister Reginald Maudling was our MP, and Thatcher was just beginning her reign in nearby Finchley. Our house was always a Labour office, and as a child my role was to fold leaflets and stuff envelopes. Later I graduated to door knocking, often with the lovely Humphrey Lyttelton who lived in our ward.

As a teenager I marched against the American war in Vietnam; later at Greenham Common, Anti-Apartheid rallies, and on CND marches with Bruce Kent.

It would never have entered my head to vote anything but Labour. I was an occasional member but often involved through unions. I always voted and supported Labour whomever the leader, it really would never have occurred to me to do anything else.

Both my animal activism and my political involvement ramped up a notch when I retired and moved back to London, living on the Isle of Dogs in the borough of Tower Hamlets. I began to see the relationship between the abuse and exploitation of animals and human exploitation. Becoming a vegan was part of that process and the exploitation of the female of all species made me understand that animal rights really is a feminist issue that needs to be explored and addressed by all activists.

The deforestation and land clearances by the multinationals, and the plundering of water supplies to feed animals for the meat and dairy industry, is a massive contributory factor to human misery and poverty.

On retiring I became a Labour member again and was able to devote a bit more time and energy to being a party member.

Then along came Jeremy Corbyn who spoke to me in a way that no other leader in my 65 years ever had. He really gave me hope that another world was possible for all the animals that inhabit this beautiful earth. What did he get though? Bitterness from some party members, ridicule by the media, MPs doing everything they could to put him down (including my own Labour MP).

Daily I began to despair. GC meetings became a nightmare, so many factions. Friends got suspended, many of us became too scared to speak out, and then of course we had the "Chicken Coup" and I will never forgive or vote for any of those that took part.

Now here we are in 2020. Battered and bruised. How do we carry on?

We do what we always do as Socialists. We are kind and have empathy for others. We must challenge every wrong-doing perpetrated by this evil government. We organise and protest and support one another.

Now, apparently, as a CND, Greenpeace and animal rights activist, I am labelled a "terrorist". It would be laughable if it wasn't so frightening, but I know the struggle for animal rights and human rights will not stop.

We will be outside the Japanese Embassy protesting the slaughter of dolphins as often as we are outside Parliament supporting refugee children being reunited with their families.

As a 70 year old New Jersey guy often says "Nobody wins unless everybody wins".

In the words of Joe Hill, "Don't mourn, organise".

Oh, and that young woman on the bus with whom I travelled home from a meeting....she is now our new Labour MP.

There is hope.

Why Not Trust the Tories?

@AndrewGodsell

Labour Party member, Aspie, Paperback Writer
Blogger with @Labour_Insider

Blog: andrewgodsell.wordpress.com

Joined Twitter 2011
5,200 Followers

A Blog from 2019, updated in 2020, to follow the continuation of dubious Tory pledges. The message from Aneurin Bevan remains relevant today, sixty years after his death. Bevan and Antonio Gramsci were major influences on my book Why NOT Trust the CONservatives?

Aneurin Bevan is famous as the Labour government minister who founded the National Health Service, which has been protecting the people since 1948. The firebrand MP for Ebbw Vale was involved in many controversies, between his first election to Parliament in 1929, and death in 1960. Less well-known are the two books that Bevan published.

In Place of Fear, from 1952, setting out the case for democratic Socialism, has been reprinted several times, without achieving the recognition accorded to many books written by former Cabinet ministers. *Why Not Trust the Tories?* was published in 1944, rapidly sold an amazing 80,000 copies, and then all but disappeared. The book has never been reprinted, and receives only passing references in biographies of Bevan.

Why Not Trust the Tories? was part of a series providing critiques of the Conservative, and right wing, approach that had dominated British politics in recent years. The most famous of these books was *Guilty Men*, by "Cato", published in 1940, attacking the appeasement of Fascism by the National Government. There was speculation that Bevan might be the author, but "Cato" was the pseudonym for a trio of journalists, including a young Michael Foot.

Four years later, Bevan did enter the literary fray. The title page of *Why Not Trust the Tories?* announced the author as "Celticus", but there was no need to speculate on the identity, as this was immediately followed by "(Aneurin Bevan, M.P.)". As a hardback, with a dust jacket, and a text running to 89 pages, this was a real book – weightier than a pamphlet. It is now 76 years since the book was published, but Bevan's work remains one of the most perceptive analyses of the negative outlook, and cynical actions, of the Conservative Party. Much of the tragedy of the past has been repeated as farce in more recent times, and Bevan's message should be heeded today.

In 1944, victory for Britain, and her allies, in World War Two was in sight. In the first chapter, "1918: After the Armistice", Bevan drew parallels with the position at the end of World War One. During both wars, Britain was governed by a coalition of the Liberal, Tory, and Labour parties. At the end of the first war, Labour decided to revert to independence, opposing the Tories.

Within days of the conflict ending, the coalition called the infamous "Coupon" General Election, with David Lloyd George, a Liberal, as Prime Minister. The Tories – shunning Liberals loyal to the preceding Prime Minister, Herbert Asquith – manoeuvred to ensure they emerged from the Election with more MPs than their partners, and thereby controlled the government moving forward. An instigator of the plan was Winston Churchill, a Liberal MP who was formerly a Tory, would later become a Tory again, and was Prime Minister at the time Bevan was writing.

In the course of the book, Bevan suggests that public opinion was shifting towards the left, and his faith was realised. Germany surrendered on May 8 1945, ending the war in Europe. Churchill wished the Coalition to continue until Japan was defeated, an event not expected to occur until the following year. Churchill was trying to repeat the trick of 1918, but Labour members of the government pressed for an early Election on party lines. During the campaign, Churchill concentrated on attacking the alleged intentions of the Labour Party, claiming that it would not be able to implement its programme without "some form of Gestapo", a sickening reference to the Nazi secret police. Churchill seemed to forget that his wartime government had included members of the Labour Party. Churchill also ignored his pre-war support of Fascism.

Labour won 393 seats, and a majority of 146, as people voted for new hope. The discredited Conservatives took only 198 seats in the 1945 Election – their smallest total between humiliating defeats by the Liberals in 1906, and Labour in 1997. The Labour Party formed its first majority government, with Clement Attlee as Prime Minister, and Bevan as Minister of Health. The Liberals experienced a long period in the wilderness, after dissolution of the coalition in 1945. They did not return to power until 2010, when a Conservative and Liberal coalition government, following that of 1918 to 1922, followed a policy of austerity, to condemn the hopes of a nation to the scrapheap.

In the second section, "The Betrayal of the Miners", Bevan looks back to 1919. With the British coal mining industry in a sorry state, due to mismanagement and profiteering by the owners, the miners argued for nationalisation and workers' control. Lloyd George, on behalf of the coalition government, set up the Sankey Commission to investigate, and Bonar Law, leader of the Tories, pledged to implement the recommendations. When the commission supported nationalisation, however, the government rapidly reneged on its promise. The coal mines remained in the hands of private owners, who were allowed to increase the price of coal, and the industry remained in crisis. Bevan noted that production dropped, from 286,000,000 tons in 1913, to 196,000,000 tons in 1943. In office from 1945, Labour carried a major programme of reform, including public ownership of the coal mines, railways, electricity, gas, and steel, plus the Bank of England.

Later conflict between the Tories and the miners led to the downfall of Edward Heath's government in 1974. Margaret Thatcher took power five years later, leading an ideological right wing government, which attacked the organised working class with deindustrialisation and privatisation. The actions of Thatcher, John Major, and David Cameron would have shocked even Bevan. The protracted miners' strike of 1984-1985 failed to reverse Thatcher's decimation of the coal industry, which was privatised in 1994, and deep coal mining in Britain completely ceased in 2015. British steel was denationalised by the Conservatives in the 1950s, renationalised by Labour in 1967, and then privatised by the Conservatives in 1988. Since 2010, the steel industry in this country, largely owned by foreign companies, has experienced a lot of uncertainty, with the Conservatives refusing suggestions that renationalisation be used to protect manufacturing capacity.

At the start of chapter three, "Death by Words", Bevan looks back to 1922, when the Tories ditched their coalition with the Liberals, which had delivered economic depression and mass

46

unemployment. The Tories won a General Election as a single party, with Law offering the country a policy of "Tranquility", which proved to be another word for cuts to services, and more unemployment. The General Election of 1922 has been echoed in 2015, as the Conservatives gained marginal constituencies from their coalition partners, the Liberal Democrats, and also Labour – funded by the Tory Electoral Fraud – and won a majority in the Commons, with only 37 per cent of the votes cast.

Bevan hops from 1922 to planning for the future, during World War Two. Tories pretended to be enthused about popular reforms, but found ways to delay their implementation. Bevan provides an excellent analysis of events surrounding the Beveridge Report, published in December 1942, which envisaged a comprehensive scheme of social security. The plan was originally due to come into effect in July 1944. The Conservative Party was not, however, enthusiastic about the scheme.

When the Beveridge Report was debated in the House of Commons, during February 1943, the Tories carried a motion welcoming it as an idea for "post-war reconstruction", defeating a backbench Labour amendment that called for "early implementation of the plan". Bevan, one of 119 MPs who voted for the amendment, writes that here was "The Tory variant of 'Jam yesterday, jam tomorrow, but never jam today'". Bevan borrowed this curious idea from Lewis Carroll's *Through the Looking Glass, And What Alice Found There*. The White Queen offered Alice work as a maid, for "Twopence a week, and jam every other day", going on to say "The rule is, jam tomorrow and jam yesterday – but never jam today".

Bevan quotes the speech by "Mr Willink, who is now Minister of Health". Henry Willink said "I am for improving the Beveridge Report", although "there are many features of the report which I do not wish to see implemented". Willink then voted with his fellow Tories for delay. During the following months, Beveridge and opposition MPs regularly pressed the government for a commitment to progress, but were met by delaying statements from Churchill and others. Bevan points out that massive public enthusiasm for the scheme was replaced by disillusion, as the Tories "contrive to drown the wistful hopes of the people for social security in a torrent of words, specious promises and endless delays".

"Jobs for Some" is the heading of Bevan's next exploration. He begins with Churchill addressing the nation in a radio broadcast, during March 1943, about post-war prospects. Bevan hears Churchill planning a repeat of 1918, with his suggestion that defeat of Hitler be followed by a Four Year Plan of reconstruction, led by "a National Government comprising the best men of all parties who are willing to serve". Bevan comments that "Political renegades always start their career of treachery as the 'best men of all parties' and end up in the Tory knackery".

A White Paper on Employment Policy arrived in May 1944, attempting to improve morale, shortly before the troops left for Normandy on D-Day. Bevan satirises the White Paper at length, particularly the idea that "thermostatic control of employment" could see troops – hoping to settle in family homes, and stable employment, upon their return after the war – being converted into mobile labourers, hopping between locations and trades, evening out fluctuations in the temperature of failing capitalism. Bevan ends the chapter with a quote from a speech he made, when the White Paper was debated in Parliament. He said of the plan, "It runs away from every major social problem. It takes refuge in tricks, strategies, and devices because it has not the honesty to face up to the implications of the social problems involved". Bevan was correct in his scepticism. Post-war Conservatism has brought continued mismanagement of the economy. The number of people unemployed rose above three million under both Thatcher, in 1982, and Major, in 1993. Cameron was little improvement in this respect, as unemployment increased to almost 2,700,000 in 2011.

"Will You Get That House?" is the question asked by the penultimate piece. Bevan remarks that while the British forces were abroad fighting the Nazis, at home the Tories were focusing on their own priority. He points out that "the private ownership of land and the right to do what they like with it have always been the holy of the holies for the Tories". From this stem issues over the provision, and affordability, of housing. Millions of new homes would have to be built to rectify a pre-war shortfall, that had been exacerbated by the destruction of bombing. Following a familiar pattern, the Tories set up a Royal Commission, and two Committees of Enquiry, rejected the suggestions they did not like, and were still procrastinating over action as Bevan completed work on the book. Bevan could not see Churchill, a Prime Minister who had the clearest power to act, delivering on his frequent promises of future "sunny uplands". In the current age, Conservative Brexiteers, of both deal and no deal persuasions, have dreamt of "sunny uplands"

— presumably overlooking headless (or chlorinated) chickens running around Brexitised wheat fields.

Britain did get a massive programme of house building after World War Two. Bevan mentions that, in 1944, Henry Willink pledged a post-war house building programme, which the former thought was far from sufficient. In practice, the man directing the programme was none other than Bevan himself, whose role as Minister of Health also included responsibility for housing. During Bevan's spell in office, a million council houses were built, to a higher quality standard than was previously in place. Council houses remained a central part of affordable housing in Britain until the decline began during the Thatcher era. The sale of council houses fuelled a growth in prices and rents plus homelessness, the sad legacy of which afflicts potential owners and tenants today, while a large proportion of current Conservative MPs are landlords.

Perhaps the most relevant part of the book for the present day is the final chapter, "The Mechanism of the Tory Mind". Bevan does not regard Tories, as men and women, to be "worse than other people". Tories have good private morals "whereas their public morals are execrable", with habitual telling of lies about their political motives. Bevan points out that "the traditional Tory does not look upon himself as the people's representative, because the Tory doctrine pre-dates the rise of modern democracy". The Tories fought against the development of democracy, and sided with Mussolini, Hitler, and Franco in their attacks on democratic government.

Bevan also draws attention to the way in which the Tories had blocked a role for Parliament in the organisation of the British economy, in order to protect their own position as the representatives of the propertied class. He states "By refusing the state effective intervention in the economic activities of society, the Tory is a potential Fascist element in the community. By denying Parliament a vigorous economic life he condemns it to death". Necessity led to an economic role for the state during the war, but Bevan pointed to signs that the Tories would seek to retain power with the help of "a freedom campaign", backed by "the Tory millionaire press", with propaganda against state regulation. This would enable a Tory to "be free once more to hunt in the jungle of economic competition". Bevan warned that the left must guard against "appearing to be the advocates of regimentation as opposed to freedom". Bevan highlighted the perennial problem for the Tories: "It is how to induce the many to vote the few back into power at each election. Or, to put it another way, how to persuade the poor to allow the rich to continue ruling". In our own day, Jeremy Corbyn has made the phrase "For the many not the few" into the Labour Party's mantra, and 2017 Manifesto title.

Tory propaganda failed in 1945, and the incoming Labour government delivered the welfare state. The defining achievement of Labour was the National Health Service, with Bevan as the architect. The Conservatives responded to the idea with vehement opposition but, with Bevan standing firm, the NHS opened on July 5 1948. On the previous day, Bevan addressed a Labour Party rally in Manchester. Having given the Tories the benefit of the doubt about their morals in 1944, he now saw things very differently, being antagonised by their attempt to block foundation of the NHS. Bevan's speech contrasted the promise of the welfare state with the poverty suffered by working class people, including himself, due to the past policies of the Conservatives. "That is why," Bevan said, "no amount of cajolery, and no attempts at ethical or social seduction, can eradicate from my heart a deep burning hatred for the Tory Party that inflicted those bitter experiences on me. So far as I am concerned, they are lower than vermin. They condemned millions of first class people to semi-starvation".

The Tory press reacted with furious condemnation, and Conservative Party members set up a Vermin Club, as a protest against Bevan. A prominent member of the club was Margaret Thatcher, an aspiring politician destined to lead a Conservative attack on the NHS decades later, with the introduction of an internal market in the 1980s.

A major reorganisation of the NHS, introduced by the Con-Dem coalition, took effect in 2013, increasing the rate at which privatisation, and fragmentation, undermined a vital public service. In 2017, Jeremy Hunt, as Secretary of State for Health, told the Conservative Party Conference: "Nye Bevan deserves credit for founding the NHS in 1948, but that wasn't him or indeed any Labour minister. That was the Conservative health minister in 1944, Sir Henry Willink, whose white paper announced the setting up of the NHS".

Many people smelt a rat, or at least a large piece of fake news. Hunt's ludicrous claim that a Conservative had set up the NHS somehow failed to deal with the fact that the Conservatives, including Willink, had voted against legislation, during 1946, that set up a comprehensive NHS – which went beyond the coalition plan of 1944. Hunt is no longer in government, having departed upon his defeat against Boris Johnson in the 2019 Conservative Party leadership election. A few months later, Johnson and the Tories won a General Election, persuading the British people that "Get Brexit Done" was the main issue. Labour's plan to end austerity, and rebuild the NHS, plus other public services, unfortunately did not win enough votes.

YOU CAN'T TRUST A WORD BORIS JOHNSON SAYS.

Lie: 40 new hospitals
Truth: 6 hospital reconfigurations

We are saddled with a Conservative government, wielding a large Parliamentary majority, and programme more extreme than Thatcherism. Johnson aims that Brexit will be followed by a trade deal with the administration of Donald Trump in the USA, which could open up the NHS to increased privatisation. Conservative General Election pledges on the NHS (plus workers' rights, and regional development) quickly proved an illusion. The Tory plan for

50,000 more nurses is a statistical con, as the figure includes retention of 18,500 nurses already working for the NHS. Johnson has repeatedly said the Conservatives will build 40 new hospitals, but the reality is funding to refurbish six existing hospitals, with hope of more work later. There has been a 17,000 reduction in the number of hospital beds under the Tories since 2010. The general increase of pressures on NHS capacity has massively intensified since the Coronavirus pandemic reached Britain.

At the start of 2020, the Johnson government carried an Act of Parliament to guarantee the highest ever cash increase in NHS funding, but in percentage terms the addition to the budget was smaller than the historic average. It also looks likely that a large amount of the extra billions of pounds for the NHS will actually find a way into private health care companies, who make donations to the Conservative Party. We always need to be wary of what the Tories say and do. The 2020 vision of the Tories seeks to repeat a cycle of deception that Bevan traced back to 1918. Why not trust the Tories? There are so many reasons!

Socialist Sunday, So Much More Than Lists and Likes

@Elaine Dyson1

Socialist into environmental issues, cats, travel, Animal rights, Glastonbury Festival & chocolate! Vegetarian. Labour & Unite Member #OpenSelection

Joined Twitter 2013
19,500 Followers

A piece written in January 2020, when asked to explain how I became a #SocialistSunday cheerleader.

I joined Twitter in 2013, but to be honest, I just didn't get it. At first, it was like being in a room full of strangers and no-one knew I was there. When I Tweeted I received one like if I was lucky, hardly surprising as I had more eggs in the fridge than followers. I gradually gave up on Twitter, my account remained open but it was abandoned in a similar way as home exercise equipment, a good idea, but rather than admit I wasn't inspired, I put it away for a while.

In 2015, a tidal wave of hope arrived in the Labour party, Jeremy Corbyn was elected as leader. My enthusiasm rose in line with my determination to support his vision and ideas.

I returned to Twitter in 2017 and soon stumbled across #SocialistSunday, a brilliant idea for connecting like-minded Socialists.

I began to follow some inspiring left-leaning folk, from the lists of names recommended. By taking part my feed changed from a chaotic mismatch of topics to one showing relevant Tweets, full of current affairs, updates, ideas and strategies, I learned so much and my follower numbers started to rise.

I then created my own list of Socialists whose Tweets really resonated with me. It was at this point my Twitter account snowballed and I began to understand how important a genre social media was in promoting Socialism and as a platform capable of cutting through the mainstream media bias, out of context soundbites and misleading newspaper headlines.

Over the last few years, #SocialistSunday has enabled many people to interact, share their ideas, inspirations, hopes and fears with like-minded Tweeters. It is much more than just a follow me and I will follow you, numbers game, but it cannot be denied a higher follower count increases Tweet exposure. Many on Twitter with a low follower count produce some excellent tweets, that disappear into cyberspace without receiving the attention they deserve, #SocialistSunday aims to rectify this.

#SocialistSunday is an opportunity to grow as a movement, a community and as a political force. I produce lists (I am only one of many) of good Socialist folk from large and small accounts and I also post a DIY follower list, where people can make their presence known by adding themselves in the reply section, without waiting to be added to someone else's list, they can then follow / follow back, each other. It's been very successful, encourages more people to get involved, to create their own lists, even if only with a handful of recommendations, to increase their reach on Twitter.

To create a list you need to copy and paste Twitter names (starting with the @ symbol) into a tweet on a Sunday, add the #SocialistSunday hashtag and post it. It's often a good idea to create the list on a Word document, or similar, as it saves time and effort in due course.

#SocialistSunday has created an inclusive community that is much more than just politics, it's where support, friendships and information exchanges flourish, enabling many to express themselves in their own way, at their own pace. It's Socialism.

Viral Socialism – We Are the Storm

Maria Roberts editor of @TheProleStar

Independent media website counteracting mainstream media bias. Watch this space – and our FB page.

Website: prole-star.co.uk

Joined Twitter 2016
21,100 Followers

A piece about the developing strength of our online community.

The "Twitterstorm" has become a valuable tool for Socialist activists online, with the creation – or appropriation – of suitable hashtags exponentially increasing our reach and ranking high in the Twitter trend charts.

It's not new – in 2015 I was privileged to be involved in the massive #NHS4XmasNo1 social media campaign, which saw the Lewisham NHS Choir topping the charts that Christmas, thanks to the concerted efforts of a team ranging from doctors and nurses to celebrities and, not least, ordinary people.

The existence of private message groups on Twitter – none of which I'm going to name here – is common knowledge. There are groups purely for chat, for specific issues or topics, and for sharing campaigning ideas. Some have become more influential than others, and these have led to the development and coordination of dozens of political campaigns.

The hugely successful #SocialistSunday hashtag came from the idea of just one person, and was initially disseminated by just a handful of Twitter accounts. Its aim was to enlarge the network of Socialist activists online, and enable them to grow their following by listing suggested accounts to connect with. Though initially coordinated, it soon snowballed and has taken on a life of its own, sustaining itself years after it first began.

#WeAreCorbyn was one of the most inspiring experiences I've ever been involved in, and though some pre-planning was done, it succeeded well beyond our wildest expectations, trending

55

worldwide for several hours on the night and all through the following day. As an exercise in solidarity, it struck the perfect note at the perfect time. It didn't change the world, but we felt exhilarated, and that we'd been part of something very important.

And not to blow our own trumpet, but social media, particularly Twitter, is somewhere we can – and do – beat the Tories hands down every time! Their ineptitude and lack of understanding of the entire phenomenon – and their apparent inability to grasp that the Internet never forgets – has created a goldmine of resources for both attack and rebuttal of their claims, and of course, a treasure trove of mockery material. There is a growing number of highly accomplished content creators, producing memes and videos from the serious to the hilarious, and most offer their material, and their advice, freely for use by others. Open source Clause 4 Socialism – in the best traditions of seizing the means of production by the efforts of hand or brain. And let's be honest – it lifts the spirits to poke fun at them!

Critics often trot out the "echo chamber" argument, saying that social media Socialists are just preaching to the converted. But they make the mistake of thinking online activists are ONLY online activists, and don't consider the many other things the majority do to campaign "in real life" as well as on social media. And it's a massive motivational help for us to connect and interact with others, share ideas and successes, console over failures – to learn from and support each other, in short.

Sadly this network we have created became very important after the General Election, when many Labour activists were shocked, despairing and badly in need of support. Some were actually saying life would not be worth living for them under another Tory government. So while Tory accounts were gloating on Twitter, Socialist accounts were reaching out to support those whose mental health was really damaged.

After the initial shock, the network has taken on another function – that of bolstering disappointed, angry campaigners to carry on. The message "Recover, Regroup, Resist" has coalesced into one simple #Resist hashtag, and the Socialist support structure has never been more vital – people are going to suffer under the Boris Johnson government, and basically, we're on our own and need to help each other. Already several groups have sprung up to help build a "real life" network of activists offering support in various ways; food and furniture banks, fuel poverty help, support for the homeless, basic household repairs to name just a few.

It's a source of bewilderment that so many online commentators have taken umbrage at the idea of social media groups organising to raise awareness of a particular issue, or to show support for individual politicians and their policies. Why the notion of Socialists working together should be considered so scandalous is a real puzzler – it's kind of a given in the entire ideology...

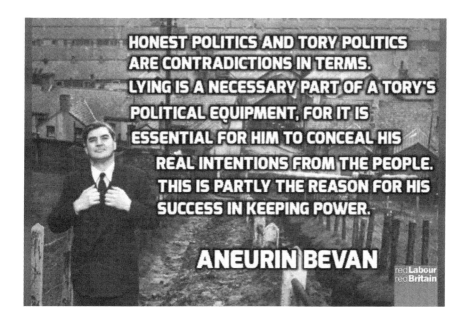

HONEST POLITICS AND TORY POLITICS ARE CONTRADICTIONS IN TERMS. LYING IS A NECESSARY PART OF A TORY'S POLITICAL EQUIPMENT, FOR IT IS ESSENTIAL FOR HIM TO CONCEAL HIS REAL INTENTIONS FROM THE PEOPLE. THIS IS PARTLY THE REASON FOR HIS SUCCESS IN KEEPING POWER.

ANEURIN BEVAN

redLabour
redBritain

After the General Election, What Do we Do?

Howard Thorp @ht4ecosocialism

Ecosocialist, writer, photographer and blogger. Environmentalist. Founder member Northwich Transition.

Blog: capitalism-creates-poverty.blogspot.com

Joined Twitter 2009
4,800 Followers

A piece from "Capitalism Creates Poverty: A Blog for the Promotion of Social, Environmental and Economic Justice", which I have been running since 2012.

Economic democracy means businesses being owned and controlled by the people who work in them. This is something we can do now and it is happening all over the world.

The beauty of worker cooperatives is that they are rooted in the local community. They don't downsize or outsource and most of the wealth they create stays in the local community boosting its health and wellbeing and quality of life. This is why everyone on the left needs to get behind building economic democracy.

So what has this got to do with the 2019 Election?

A lot.

We are now faced with another five years of Tory government and probably a hard Brexit. The assault on the unemployed and disabled will continue. Rough sleeping will continue to grow. The economy will struggle and may go into recession. There will continue to be a hostile environment for migrants and nothing will be done about the climate crisis.

To deal with this we need a two-pronged approach working to elect a radical Labour government in 2024, and building community support from the grassroots upwards.

At a community level, this means mutual aid – solidarity not charity. But it isn't just about providing food, clothing, and shelter for the victims of this government.

It's about creating meaningful jobs and building homes. It's about recreating and rebuilding the commons. We can do these things ourselves and it's already happening.

To really make this take off we need help. Finance is a major issue. Whilst some projects can be realised through crowdfunding others will require financial support.

This is where local councils come in, and despite the fact that they have had budgets slashed by the Conservatives there are still many things that councils can do to support local groups and build community wealth, which is why it's important to elect as many Labour councillors as possible.

We need to ensure that councils are following, where possible, the "Preston Model" of community wealth building. This has been successfully developed, since 2012, by Preston City Council and the Centre for Local Economic Strategies.

Councils can also help in the fight against the climate crisis. They can improve public transport systems and pedestrianise town centres. They can improve local recycling facilities, rewild council land, build energy-efficient housing and help set up community energy companies powered by green energy.

One example of community action is CAG Oxfordshire, summarised as follows on their website:

Community Action Group (CAG) Oxfordshire consists of over 70 groups across Oxfordshire, at the forefront of community led climate change action, organising events and projects to take action on issues including waste, transport, food, energy, biodiversity and social justice.

Started in 2001, the network is the largest of its kind in the UK, running over 2,000 events per year, attended by around 80,000 local residents and contributing over 20,000 volunteer hours to the county.

This government isn't going to help us so we need to get together and help ourselves. We can do it and make a positive difference in people's lives. We still also need to work and campaign at national and regional level to put pressure on the government, and get Labour elected the next time around.

There's a lot to do but we can do it. Let's get on with it.

The Future Direction of the Labour Party
Following the 2019 General Election

Michael Lewis @michael75lewis

Member of @prospectunion @gmb_union @cnduk @amnestyUK
@libertyhq & @UKLabour
Support @votesat16 @electoralreform @GreenpeaceUK
#BDS #Palestine #SaveOurSteel

Joined Twitter 2017
1,300 Followers

Thoughts about our structure and policy going forward, prompted by the party leadership contest in the early part of 2020.

In 2015, Jeremy Corbyn was overwhelmingly elected as the new leader of the Labour Party, bringing left-wing politics back to the mainstream and giving hope to Socialist movements around the world. The UK's official opposition now had a Socialist leader who had a thumping majority over his rivals in the first round of the leadership ballot.

Fast-forward four years, and Labour lost the 2019 General Election in a way that no Socialist could ever imagine possible, but it was not the fault of the leader Jeremy Corbyn or Socialist leaning members of the parliamentary party that lost this election. It was hate, fear, bigotry, lies, slander and likely fraud that won this election for the Conservative Party.

The state controlled media, the right-wing press, the ultra-right-wing Conservatives, UKIP, and the Brexit Party, plus the centre-right faction within the Labour Party contributed to four years of misinformation against the leader of the opposition. Combined with confusion over the Brexit policy, and the Parliamentary lock-jam caused by Theresa May's 2017 General Election, this led to the biggest electoral defeat for the Labour Party since 1935.

Jeremy Corbyn, at his own election count, announced that he would stand down as leader. It was time to choose the next Labour Party leader and deputy leader. This essay is a plea to the new leadership, to take the massive advances that have been made to Socialist policy between 2015 and 2019 and develop this into not only an effective Socialist opposition, but also a strong alternative programme for government. The next Labour government should hit the ground running on day one, to be as reforming as (if not more so) as Clement Attlee's 1945-1951 government.

I believe any leader or deputy leader of the Labour Party must:

•   Be a MP with a proven track record in Parliament and in representing their constituents.

•   Have Socialist values, after all Labour is a Socialist party. Must be committed to public ownership of vital services and utilities.

•   Have held roles in either the Cabinet or Shadow Cabinet, or have been a Select Committee chair or be a senior member of Parliament. Experience is key!

•   Be representative of the Labour movement and the UK electorate and always be an inclusive leader. And the leadership team must always have a female in it, either as leader or as deputy leader.

•   Be a dyed-in-the-wool Parliamentarian who believes in democracy and local community involvement.

I would suggest having two deputy posts, one of which is exclusively reserved for females, with the following structure:

Deputy Leader (1) – should be responsible for party structure and discipline (this would be a Cabinet post possibly the Duchy of Lancaster). The Chief Whip would work closely with the post holder.

Deputy Leader (2) – should be responsible for membership and community engagement (again this should be a Cabinet post possibly a newly created Secretary of State for the Home Nations, bringing the Departments for Scotland, Wales, Northern Ireland and the Department for Housing, Communities and Local Government into this new role, which would champion all areas of the four nations).

I have been a committed Labour supporter since early childhood. In 1983, I was 7 years old and helping local Labour Councillors to get out the vote at the General Election as my school was closed for the day. I have helped out at elections whenever I can, and although I may not have agreed with all policies or have voted for all of the leadership and deputy leadership candidates who eventually won, my support for Labour has never wavered. I even considered standing for election as a Councillor twice, first in 2005 and again in 2008.

The Tony Blair and Gordon Brown governments achieved some great things, but they were not radical enough! Gordon Brown was so underrated, unfortunately, he had the media turn against him. A snap election in 2007 could have altered history.

While Blair and Brown did great work with redistributing income, the National Childcare Strategy, Sure Start, the National Minimum Wage, devolution, and the Good Friday Agreement (to name a few), they did get things wrong too.

Disenfranchisement began many decades ago, but the social media age and unpopular policies helped it to spread like a common cold. This disenfranchisement led to ten years of austerity, Brexit and Boris Johnson as Prime Minister which is an absolute disaster for the UK.

Labour needs a campaigning leader and deputy leader, who will take the Socialist cause to every community and who will take on the vile, right-wing propaganda machine (commonly known as the press).

Socialism isn't a dirty word, it is a set of values, a belief system based on sharing and state ownership. Socialists can win power, but we need to convince people that it is a radical alternative to this extremely right-wing government.

A Socialist UK government should commit to:

1) Nationalised utilities and essential services: gas, electricity, water and broadband, the police, prisons, NHS, schools, universities and social care should be provided by the state. New social housing must be built and empty properties turned into suitable social housing.

2) A national living wage of £15.00 per hour, increasing by the real cost of living each April, the rate must apply to everyone aged 16

63

and above. If an apprenticeship rate must be retained, then this must be equivalent to at least 50% of the national living wage.

3) A universal income of at least £1,000 per month, per adult. This would involve removing most benefits, but it would also allow scope for enhancing the state pension, and disability benefits. A complete review of benefits and support needs to be undertaken in opposition so that legislation can be laid out in the first Queen's Speech.

4) A progressive income and corporation tax system, with income tax and national insurance thresholds aligned and starting at £15,000 a year (again increasing each year by the real cost of living). Tax rates should be tiered at 5%, 10%, 15%, 20%, 25%, 30%, 35%, 40%, 45% and 50%. Corporation tax should be aligned with countries in the EU 27. Workers', environmental and human rights must be aligned with Europe.

5) Establish a commission to look at a new future for the UK monarchy, with the aim of considering all options for this institution. Introduce a written constitution, which sets out how the UK is governed.

6) Introduce Single Transferable Vote (STV) for all UK elections – it works in Northern Ireland and we use a multitude of systems in the rest of the UK, standardise them all to STV and abandon First Past the Post to the history books once and for all.

7) Abolish the House of Lords and replace it with a fully elected Senate. Fixed-terms of 4 years for the Commons and Senate with elections taking place every two years, Senate then two years later the Commons. Limit the Prime Minister's tenure to 8 years.

8) Return power to the people, introduce people's assemblies, hold local and national referendums to inform policy (not to hi-jack or dictate policy as in the case of Brexit).

9) Restructure all local authorities, so that each area has effective multi-tier local government, health boards, transport authorities and devolved assemblies with clearly defined roles. The Department for the Home Nations would lead on this.

10) Abolish academy trusts and bring all state schools back into local authority control.

11) Reintroduce Sure Start, devise a new national childcare strategy, ban the sale of school fields. Reintroduce Educational Maintenance Allowance and pay it directly to all 16-19 year olds in education.

12) Abolish Police and Crime Commissioners and use more community based and restorative justice sentences. Prison should be a last resort not a default position.

13) Bring the NHS back into full public ownership, invest significantly in the NHS, scrap prescription charges and parking charges.

14) Develop a National Care Service that provides fully funded social care from birth to end of life care. Restore funeral grants.

15) Introduce a National Education Service that covers pre-school, compulsory schooling, FE, HE and lifelong learning, which should be free. Charge VAT on private school fees.

16) Introduce automatic voter registration, link this to issuing of National Insurance numbers. Reduce voting age to 16. Consider merging all identifying numbers into just one – possibly the individual's NHS number – this would make it easier for people to remember, there would be no need for a separate National Insurance number, hospital numbers, driving license or passport numbers. This one number would confirm identity quickly and easily.

17) Scrap Trident, work towards complete nuclear disarmament and strengthen the peace-keeping roles of NATO and the UN in mediating between warring countries.

18) Develop a clear strategy for political funding requirements and strengthen electoral law, consider state funding for political parties.

19) The UK is a diverse country, we need to foster strong community relations and that starts in our own party. We need a policy statement on accepting all who share our values, this statement must deal with all forms of discriminatory behaviour. We also need disciplinary procedures that work. We are an anti-racist, anti-homophobic, anti-sexism, anti-ageism, anti-oppression, anti-bias party.

20) Develop a strategy for bringing rail and bus transport back into public ownership and link this in with a green strategy to become carbon neutral and rely solely on green energy. In the late 1980s and early 1990s I was campaigning for green policies, fast forward 30 years and the climate change of my youth has become a climate emergency – ACTION IS REQUIRED NOW.

The path the power is going to be long, hard work and there will be challenges, but it is vital that our leadership team start the process of radical reform now. This country is desperate for a Labour government. Please use your campaigns to grow our movement and to show the world that Socialism is a valid value base and one that can govern effectively introducing radical reforms.

Good luck!

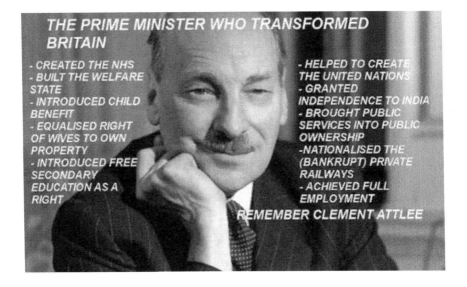

THE PRIME MINISTER WHO TRANSFORMED BRITAIN

- CREATED THE NHS
- BUILT THE WELFARE STATE
- INTRODUCED CHILD BENEFIT
- EQUALISED RIGHT OF WIVES TO OWN PROPERTY
- INTRODUCED FREE SECONDARY EDUCATION AS A RIGHT

- HELPED TO CREATE THE UNITED NATIONS
- GRANTED INDEPENDENCE TO INDIA
- BROUGHT PUBLIC SERVICES INTO PUBLIC OWNERSHIP
- NATIONALISED THE (BANKRUPT) PRIVATE RAILWAYS
- ACHIEVED FULL EMPLOYMENT

REMEMBER CLEMENT ATTLEE

Solidarity with Karie Murphy

@Rachael_Swindon

Persistent, Blocked by 87 Tory MPs & Right Said Fred, Growing interest in politics, Bad driver, Mum, I swear, I blog a bit, GTTO.

Joined Twitter 2014
77,600 Followers

I'm not particularly great at talking about me, hence I've turned down a fair few interview things over the last few years. I managed to battle the Daily Mail *with help from Karie Murphy, who herself came under media attack in early 2020.*

Rachael x

PS, I think the Get the Tories Out! *book is a great idea. The book is an excellent read, meticulously focused on grassroots activists. It is really interesting for activists like me to see what others do, and this collates it nicely. And I'm pleased my GTTO tag gets to live on!*

I'm not much of a thread writer, but I'll make an exception here, because I've seen some of the stuff said about "Corbyn firewall", Karie Murphy, and it simply isn't the woman I know, and it needs correcting.

So allow me to put some facts in to the conversation.

I first became "known" in 2015. I had no affiliation with the Labour Party. I was happily Tweeting my little homemade memes, getting blocked by one Tory MP after another. Jeremy Corbyn was a man you'd see on the news sometimes, usually criticising foreign policy. When I saw what Jeremy had to say, I was on board, and I Tweeted in support of Jeremy and the Labour Party. By the 2017 General Election I was getting 2-3 million impressions of my Tweets, every day. This made me a target for some of the right-wing press.

A few months after the election, I was "doorstepped" by a reporter from the *Daily Mail*. He had spent several weeks trying to locate me, trying to get dirt on me from neighbours, it was pretty sinister stuff. The reporter chased me down the road, calling my name.

He upset me, and he upset my family, it's not something we're familiar with. Despite what you might think, I am literally just a normal mum. When he left I was a wreck, I wondered what rubbish he would write about me. Then enter Karie Murphy.

Prior to this, I knew her name. I remember her coming to prominence when the "Chicken Coup" MPs, including Starmer and Nandy, performed some pathetic coordinated mass resignations in an attempt to remove Jeremy Corbyn.

Karie Murphy was the glue that bound the spine of the Corbyn book. Without Murphy, Corbyn would've been gone in 2016. Of course, the media version is very different, but I can assure you, Karie Murphy took the fury of the PLP so Jeremy could do his job.

Anyway... A few hours after a couple of left wing media outlets wrote about my doorstepping incident, out of nowhere came a message from Karie Murphy, asking if me and my "wee bairns" were OK. I thought it was wind up, I was still pretty panicked from the *Mail*'s inquisition.

A mutual friend sent Karie my number after Karie asked her if there was any way she could get in touch with me. She was genuinely concerned for me and my family, I kind of got the impression she knew what it was like to be harassed by the media.
She also thanked me for all of the effort I put in. Despite what people thought, I've never been on the Labour payroll, I've only ever done this because I want to.

I asked Karie if there was anything I could do to stop the *Mail* harassing me, or publishing false stories.

Karie gave me the email address of a guy called Howard, and within half an hour I had an email from Howard, to send on to the editor of the *Daily Mail*, telling them to leave me the fuck alone, but in legal language, obviously.

Soon after, the *Mail* confirmed they wouldn't be bothering me again.

I cannot put in to words the relief I felt, it was a bloody horrible experience, made that bit easier by the compassion and decency of Karie Murphy. Nobody else from the party ever bothered.

The day after it all kicked off, Karie messaged me again, just to make sure I was OK. In jest, I said "nothing that a Christmas card from Jeremy couldn't fix". Soon after, a personal card came from Jeremy Corbyn, apparently he'd heard of me

Since then, I've heard from Karie quite often, she probably felt a bit sorry for me. But it was always to ask if I was OK. She is an incredibly caring lady. I've met lots of different people through the Labour movement, but hand on heart, Karie Murphy is one of the best. I learnt through MSM she once donated a kidney to a complete stranger, and that kind of sums her up perfectly.

I've had a cup of tea with her once. My kids thought she was fantastic, she asked them what they wanted to do when they left school. She took an interest. They both ask how she is often. Kids are usually a good judge of character.

There's many more examples I can give you of the kind of person she is. She has steadfast Socialist principles, she doesn't suffer fools, she cares about people, she hates Tories more than me.

Some of the stuff I've read is beyond the pale. I've seen media attacks launched on her while she was burying her mother. And the attacks were briefed by a former high profile Labour MP that knew she was burying her mother. Sick bastard.

I have seen her character assassinated on a weekly basis. I have seen blatant lies made up about her. Anyone that takes this much on the chin must have something worth saying, and the powerful do not like it, just like they didn't like Mr Corbyn.

So I stand by Karie Murphy, because she stood by me when others couldn't care less. She is a decent human being, believe me, or believe Murdoch and Co, it's your choice really, but stop attacking a woman based on what you've read in the papers. Duh.

Solidarity with Karie Murphy and the team that have supported her and Jeremy for the last few years, you know who you are. You're all stars.

Ten Pledges to End the Leadership Crisis for Labour

Catherine @catheri82106796

Grandmother.
Trying to save the planet and end war by replacing neo-capitalism with something nicer.

Blog: kaygreen.blog

Joined Twitter 2012
4,100 Followers

I didn't like the Ten Pledges from the Board of Deputies of British Jews our leadership candidates were signing up to, during January 2020. So I wrote my own Ten Pledges, and put them on my Blog. Within days, my little one-woman blog had THOUSANDS of shares and reads, and then some bigger Blogs gave them a boost. They are now OUR Ten Pledges.

Here are ten pledges the Labour leadership contenders might like to sign up to.

1 Resolve outstanding cases

Many members are hampered in their political activities by the lingering uncertainty of what they suspect are vexatious, politically motivated complaints. We are a well-funded organisation. If you haven't got the staff, please employ some to get these cases looked at speedily and, where not justified, thrown out.

2 Make the party's disciplinary process independent

That is, make sure *our* process *is* independent. Stop taking instructions from organisations that have, one way or another, managed to present as the uncontested voice of people who don't necessarily agree with them, and please endeavour to stop MPs being fooled by such organisations.

3 Ensure transparency

Tell the membership what is going on, who is dealing with what, and under which rules, and how members can make their views heard.

Give the membership, and your staff, full and easily accessed details of how complaints, disciplinary actions and hearings work, and who exactly is dealing with them. Never let it be suspected that agencies with special access are hearing about, or influencing, actions that affect members, without those members knowing about it.

4 Prevent re-admittance of prominent offenders

Resist giving Shadow Cabinet posts or other power positions to MPs or execs who have repeatedly briefed against the party and / or the manifesto in ways that clearly go against the members' wishes, or who have seriously misrepresented or slandered the membership.

5 Provide no platform for bigotry

Bigotry means disrespect for, or abuse aimed at, others whose ideas disagree with yours.

Do not let anyone with a powerful voice in the party demand the silencing or no-platforming of members, former members, or citizens generally, unless those individuals are clearly breaking the law by, for example, inciting violence.

On the other hand, on no account name or label individuals you happen to disagree with in a way that encourages the public to see them as "fair game" for abuse or disrespect, especially don't do this just because you don't want views that challenge your own heard.

6 Adopt the universal definitions of racism, sexism and classism

Don't let anyone tell you that racism means anything other than what the dictionary says it does, and don't let one group's definitions or concerns endanger minority groups by crowding out all others.

7 Deliver an anti-racism education programme, and an anti-sexism one, and an anti-classism one and, while you're at it, an anti-corruption one

Deliver anti-racism, anti-sexism and anti-classism education that makes sense to members, particularly those who are themselves significantly disadvantaged by those attitudes.

8 Engage with the membership, and with the people of this country, as efficiently and as directly as you can.

When you engage with "the community" please take some time to work out exactly who you are engaging with, and what actual proportion of the actual people in this country you are dealing with. If it turns out to be a strangely small number of voices speaking for a larger group, do some research and try again.

9 Communicate with resolve

Bland, generic statements should give way to actively telling people what is – and isn't – going on in the party, and why. When the membership go wrong, tell them straight. When the membership are slandered and falsely accused, rebut the accusations and support the membership.

10 Show leadership and take responsibility

If we have a leader who does not do so, powerful organisations will take charge and dictate to them against the interests of the membership.

Our Socialist Struggle Must Continue

Beck Robertson @punkishunicorn

Writer. Journalist. Economic Socialist. Labour Party Member. Bad ass copywriter for hire.

Joined Twitter 2019
300 Followers

At the start of 2020, I suggested this detailed left strategy to win the argument for Socialism.

The recent election result dealt a heavy blow to many of us on the Socialist left. Since December 12, spurious column inches have been dedicated to what went wrong, with self-appointed pundits situated squarely in the political centre, now emboldened enough to insist Socialism is unpalatable to the British electorate.

Sweeping Socialist economic reform that would benefit the vast majority of people, is not, however, what went wrong. In fact Socialism is *precisely* the kind of radical change the country, weary of the neoliberal status quo, is crying out for. If Brexit had been over with, it's fair to say, Johnson's 80 seat majority would not have happened.

We must not now sit back and lick our wounds but cement our solidarity and struggle on. The question of course, is *how*, what must we do to ensure the next election is ours?

The answer lies in the heartlands we lost, and in the ones we retained. Grassroots activism is the surest way of building solid support, as it enables a movement to grow organically, and ensures policy reflects public opinion.

We must take politics to the people, pry it from the dusty halls of Westminster and set up Socialist centres of activism in the heart of towns and cities around the UK.

We must show we are willing to engage and *listen* to people living in the communities we want to win the support of, and we must demonstrate two points clearly – the first, that we intend to represent people's wishes, and the second, we seek their permission to implement the kind of change that will make a measurable, positive difference to their lives.

To win, Labour must paint a picture that immediately tells a story. It's one thing having the kind of policies that will alter this country for the better, another to be able to weave a narrative that illustrates what that world will look like.

The communicators of our project's message must be able to make people aspire, imagine, and crave the world we aim to build. People must believe this world is entirely possible, so the ground must be primed in advance.

We should not overwhelm, but outline some core goals clearly, possibly using an easy-to-refer to pledge card, that can be distributed both on and offline. Voters must see how we will directly benefit them, *as individuals*, as this is by far the quickest way to get people to take action.

A pledge card that can be used to quickly illustrate our primary goals should cover aims like the following:

1) Democratise and reform political representation to empower people to see politics not as something out of reach, but something they can actively engage in.

2) Free Education as a right, from birth to the grave, as only through education can people become empowered to shape the world they live in.

3) Sparklingly efficient public services, run for the people and owned in their trust.

4) A humane welfare system that ensures essential economic provision for all, on a sliding scale, to each according to his or her need.

5) Unprecedented healthcare investment, fully funded by higher taxes levied on those fortunate enough to be benefiting from our exploitative capitalist system.

This is the world the elite do not want us to build, for they have far too much of a stake in the creaking old order. We can beat them, we can have people power on our side, for the current status quo is not benefitting the majority of working class people.

The faults of the current system, and the inevitable failure of the Tories to deliver on election pledges, made to the communities whose votes they coasted to power on, are precisely the reason why we must go local and grassroots. We should hold open political forums, where we encourage all residents to attend, ask Labour questions, and tell us their concerns.

We *must* be open to what people say, and we must show them we have listened, by reflecting common concerns and issues in our policy. The 2019 manifesto was amazing, the next can be even better, a living manifesto literally written by the people, for the people.

We must harness the full power of the unions by encouraging all workers to mobilise and agitate for fairer pay, and better working conditions. We must do this using the language of aspiration, and supercharge this by tapping into the anger many rightfully feel at their economic lot, a "what you should have as your fair share" approach, rather than an unceasing picture of doom.

We should amplify publicly the already strong link between Labour and the unions, so the working class electorate knows instinctively who is on their side, and who is on the side of exploitative capitalists.

There is a great need to create spaces of activism in communities where people from all walks of life can participate in local politics. By doing this we will give people exactly what they want, control over policy, a feeling their voice is being heard.

Our party is broad and beautiful, our aims are truly inspirational. Our first task must be to unite under a Socialist banner, as only Socialism can deliver the changes that are so needed. Our second task must be to immediately begin engaging with those outside our Labour family.

There is much positive difference a Socialist Labour government would make, if Corbyn had been elected, by 2025, we would be living in a transformed country. No one reliant on foodbanks to survive, no exploitative zero hours contracts, no exhaustive NHS queues, and no one without a home. It's our job to illustrate this world and to do this we must cut through the lies of mainstream media, which exists only to serve the interests of the elitists.

The path to power is not to opt for a media friendly safe man or woman who plans to keep things almost exactly the same, with a few meagre crumbs thrown here or there. This would be a sure-fire route to disaster, the public are already tired of the status quo, as evidenced by Brexit, by offering nothing different we will *never* inspire.

The answer to the media's incessant slander, is to implant ourselves so firmly in local communities and serve them, that we become trusted friends of the people, not hectoring, lofty remote symbols.

It would be prudent to build and invest in alternative robust media that can be widely read and shared. Socialist papers that already exist and have established a circulation should be strengthened, such as the *Morning Star*, new media sites must be supported and founded.

Community newsletters could be established as well, to inform people of the most relevant political issues on their doorstep, distributed to their door. This approach could form a key part of our campaign to raise awareness of the Tories' inevitable shortcomings in people's local districts.

Paired with a strategy to encourage community participation in shaping Labour's politics, this would pave the way for certain electoral success, well before any election took place.

The burst of energy that came from Labour activists, people who had volunteered their time freely, did not come from nowhere. It came from a deep passion for a cause that connected, our job now is to inspire the same excitement in the broader electorate.

Encouraging people to get involved at the local level, *irrespective of whether they are a member of the party or not*, is an excellent way of establishing trust and reconnecting.

Making it easier for people to join the party is another obvious, yet often overlooked, way to make people a part of our movement. We should be encouraging more working class people to join Labour, not just online, which can be a somewhat isolating environment, but in their communities.

We must demonstrate why joining Labour is in their interests, by outlining how our policies will benefit people specifically, but also by emphasising the say members get over the shaping of party politics, and by making our fee structure and application process even more accessible.

There is also a need to refine some of our internal processes to make them faster and more democratic so they allow us to adapt quicker to input from potential voters, as well as the views of the majority of members. We should not aim to be governed by a few sitting at the top, but instead be led by the many voices positioned at the bottom.

On issues of foreign policy our message must align with our domestic policies. We stand against capitalist exploitation, and warmongering for profit, we stand against bigotry, we stand for equality for all. There is absolutely no reason we cannot state a position that supports the freedom of the Palestinian people yet stands firmly against anti-Semitic bigotry, we must take this position, and not renege on our principles.

Where we can integrate with initiatives that tangibly seek to improve people's lives under this brutal Tory government, we must do so. We should not shy away from creating, supporting, or getting involved with food banks, running local single issue campaign groups, or enmeshing ourselves in other charity drives.

Nor should we hide our involvement in such initiatives. These, after all, are the issues that matter, by showing how we embody our political worldview, even without the power of governance, we'll be demonstrating ahead of the game how we put ideals into action.

Raising awareness of class politics is another essential. Currently, our society is divided up into the haves, and the have nots, our job is not to err on the side of caution, so we do not frighten the haves, who for the most part, do not currently have the motivation to change the system they benefit from.

Fortunately, or unfortunately, depending on how you look at it, we have the numbers on our side – the have nots vastly outnumber the haves. Millions living on the breadline, millions more unemployed or underpaid, terminally ill patients denied life-saving essential medication, thousands of people homeless on the streets.

Sadly, in the last Election, the message got lost. Many of the have nots opted for a government that will not serve them, due to a number of factors. One of these factors was our inability to cut through in time, amid all the Tory spin and media lies. This time around the campaign must begin immediately, building a power base community by community. Then we must link it all together with an overarching, clearly articulated strategy to transform Britain for the better.

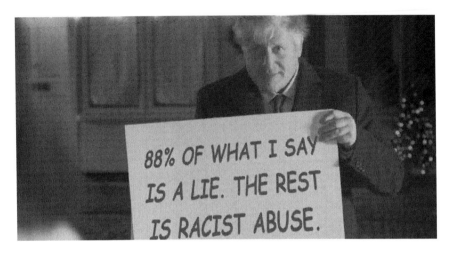

By putting people in touch with political power, by offering them a practical way to challenge the elitist exploiters who keep them down, we will ignite the spark of Socialist revolution.

This is where class politics comes in, most people are aware it's one rule for the rich, and another for the poor but our country has lingered so long on neoliberal economics they cannot quite imagine the vehicle that will get them to a world where they benefit. Labour are that vehicle. A big part of our narrative should seek to emphasise just how capitalism seeks to oppress all but the very few. Economics may not be sexy, but it is essential to people's lives.

Anger and disgruntlement should be employed, and directed to positive ends. We saw how potent a weapon anger could be when it was so skilfully weaponised by Dominic Cummings, during both the 2016 Leave and 2019 Election campaigns. Cummings though, only has purposeless anger and lies, yet those lies connect because sometimes Socialists have been too afraid to show their teeth.

Anger might sound contradictory to the language of aspiration but the two are most effective when used hand in hand. The worker has a right to get angry about conditions that prevent him or her from aspiring for more, the more they are entitled to for their hard labour.

In our currently divided society, people are already angry, but presently, they have nowhere yet to put it that will benefit them. Brexit allowed the Tories to define themselves as the voice of the unheard, yet they are a one trick pony, devoid of the ability to deliver any positive change to the majority of these people's lives.

However the aftermath of Brexit pans out, and under a Tory government it will likely not be pretty, one thing is for certain. The parasite that is the capitalist exploiter will continue, long after we leave the EU.

By focusing on class politics, and solid Socialist economics, we can sweep away the Tories paper-thin promises come the next Election. We can only do this though, if we begin now to reconnect with the worker, as well as those unemployed because of austerity. We can only do this if we pick up our shattered hope, and start once again on our march to Socialist victory.

There should be no hesitation. After all, we have both truth, and the solution, in our armoury.

Lenin wrote "Despair is typical of those who do not understand the causes of evil, see no way out, and are incapable of struggle". The words are from a 1910 newspaper piece, *L N Tolstoy and the Modern Labour Movement*. During 2020, and moving forward, we must not despair, but fight the good fight, for another world is well within our grasp.

Labour in Check-Mate – The Political Vagrancy of the Working Class

Mandy Clare @Mandy4Dene

Working Class activist and mum.
Lifelong Socialist.
Enough of the cruelty & embedded inequality.

Joined Twitter 2011
1,000 Followers

A piece I wrote in the early stages of the Labour leadership election, featured on the "Labour Heartlands" website.

Within the Labour Party membership, we have so much more to say about Palestine, the environment, or the trans debate than we do about the enforced political vagrancy of our own working class communities and voices.

Does this mean those other more dominant issues don't matter or that we should not speak up or debate them? No, not at all. But do we make ourselves irrelevant and alienating to our traditional Labour-voting heartlands by obsessing over them in comparison with the lived realities, injustices and political invisibility of our own working class within the U.K.? Yes we do. There is no equalities protection in law for the politically voiceless working class.

There is no earnest discussion, or outrage, about class discrimination or social cleansing, early death and prolonged morbidity of the working class, within the political education of "The World Transformed". When a rare workshop with class in the subject heading has been held, the issue has been pontificated on mainly by middle class academics and high profile media names, with scant depth or sociological analysis applied and invariably been swiftly hijacked back onto the equalities areas the middle class left find more palatable and relatable – trans, race, gender, disability. Often in that order.

If we are looking at this purely from the point of view of proportional representation – working class invisibility within this party is by far the bigger issue, but the reality is, we aren't interested and it doesn't fire us up. We can't relate. It threatens us.

The middle class majority on the left seem to have much more of a comfortable familiarity with the issues of other minority or disempowered groups than with the working class. It seems they are far more willing to get on board and be vocal on those issues. Perhaps it's tedious having to listen to inarticulate people suggesting your personal success is based on networks and privilege. You came here to be outraged about something – a pet confined injustice or two, to which you know all the answers and with a vague idea of Socialism being about becoming kinder to the poor, helping them be more like you and having more of the material things you have, but not really wanting to be told you are part of their problem, or that power within the party needs to be effectively turned on its head.

Some activists call for an end to all identity politics as if by waving that magic wand, the social structures formed of deep prejudice and hoarding of power through history and the social inequality it produces will suddenly be swept away if we stop talking about it. Actually, language is one of the few weapons we have to bring it repeatedly out into the open so that it can be challenged. Silence that and the power imbalances remain and further entrench. Besides, class can't be included within the identity politics bracket. Every other strand you might want to look at has legal recognition, protection and a movement behind it. A legion of middle class activists, usually. The working class enjoy no such protection, recognition or vocal solidarity, hence their alienation and political vagrancy. That can't be remedied by simply ignoring it further.

We have a problem. The election result has spooked our MPs into talking a little bit more about the "working class" as opposed to the sociologically vacuous "working people". I get it – the blander catch-all is meant to include "both wings" of the party – the heartlands vote share and the Blair loyal, plus the newer middle class Corbyn influx, but the problem with that is one of those wings has been so neglected and disempowered within this party that it has detached itself. In addition, reintroduction of the terms "working class" and "heartlands" hasn't yet led to any affirmation of the extent of our failings on this issue. We have had vague references to how the last 40 years have led us to the final crumbling of the "Red Wall", but no firm commitments as to how we fix that within our party, structurally.

I want to see a party that can connect with the working class genuinely, not through vague soundbites, because it's easy to say these things to win votes and sound cool, then do nothing once elected and that is one of the main reasons working class trust began draining away from Labour under Blair and hasn't returned – in all honesty, they just can't be bothered with us and see us as all the same. Who can blame them? I want to see a party that is supportive of and trusted by the working class, because it values them and actually elevates their voice. Imagine the difference if those in positions of power within this party actually put themselves face to face with class-based prejudice, named it and took it on. Imagine the respect that would generate. The working class want to "come back home" but no one wants to be where they are just used and are not valued and accepted for who they are. That's not a home, really. It's this party that has got this wrong and that needs to change.

Race is important. The working class is multi-ethnic and the class barriers apply across the board in a similar way in terms of basic access to routes to power and voice. Protections and measures put in place have resulted in a significant increase in BAME representation overall but with the combined barrier of social class in the mix, activists are going to struggle much more to be taken seriously and access support to become a candidate than if from a more privileged background. Especially if operating from your own class voice and identity. This is true across the board also. One key difference between working class broad ethnic groups occurred during this General Election in that the working class BAME vote went predominantly to Labour – very possibly because of the fear that a Hard Brexit might herald another racist backlash toward their communities, which is appalling.

The Daily Heil, Scum and other poisonous outlets winding up nationalistic sentiment in Boris' favour won't have had the same reach and ability to stoke feelings of injustice in the way it did within the white working class, but the point is, the white working class sense of loss does have some basis in reality. This party used to belong to the working class. The unions used to be a vehicle for the working class. These were the only political voice and element of power that they had.

If Labour had not moved so far away from the working class in general, parachuting southern middle class MPs into northern safe seats and then failing to address the snub under Corbynism, the political vagrancy of the white working class and their sense of betrayal would not have been so easy for the gutter media and Johnson to corral. In this regard, we left an open goal for them to exploit.

There are too many within our own membership all too ready to write off the working class as inherently ignorant and racist. Racism exists in all social classes, but to understand why there has been a resurgence within the heartlands, we need to pay attention to these dynamics, and our part in it historically and now. It isn't lost on Dominic Cummings, being the Tories' man on the inside, who was able – because of his class insight, and helped by our class ignorance – to very easily give Johnson a steer on how to capitalise on our abject failure over decades on class, using the white working class as pawns in a game of chess.

We may have had one isolated working class voice within our leadership team, amongst the clamour of how many pressing for policies that would appeal to the middle class at the expense of the last remaining scraps of heartlands trust? We are responsible, through our long-term arrogance and neglect, for our own Check-Mate. The whole, multi-ethnic, working class loses, ultimately, as a result of our class-blinkered failure.

Internationalism is important. I studied sociology and social divisions of power not just within the UK or modern capitalist Western economies but also between First and Third World. How those power divisions came to exist and are maintained and expanded is endlessly relevant to our fight against social injustice here and overseas as the divisions intensify under relentless capitalism.

So we have a lot to gain at some point from a proper go at uniting the international working class. I would be the first to say it. We don't want to see people paddling across the bloody English / French channel for 11 hours straight just to gain their right to asylum. We need a calm, respectful and productive conversation about many things – immigration, the implications of the Gender Recognition Act, global aid and the impacts of structural adjustment and trade blocks, how we value care work and parenting, the military industrial complex, the environmental crisis.

There are loads of things to sort out, if and when we win power – fine. But we need to embed working class voices within how we shape that discussion now and ensure our pitch to the nation reflects the society we live in next time. To be credible, we also need to enable our working class activists to shine and achieve within our ranks. There are so many barriers standing in the way. We can't assume what they are, any more than we would assume what barriers bar the way to full participation and being taken seriously, for women, BAME or other under-represented members – we need to ask those working class activists who have shown willing, as a starting point "what have we got wrong?". Class discrimination and invisibility in positions of power and in politics generally is a wider social problem which extends beyond our party but we should be leading the way and starting with our own systems and activists. It is amazing to me that this needs pointing out within a Socialist party.

We need to recognise how irrelevant we sometimes come over to working class voters. Our pet issues may be laudable and justified but totally off the radar for most working class people against the backdrop of job insecurity and rising living costs, against no savings and a social safety net shot to pieces, against decades of being side-lined and ignored, looked down upon by the middle class political elite, busy concerning themselves with fixing, understanding and empathising with everything under the sun apart from what's on their own doorstep.

We can improve by taking each of those pet issues and considering where they may figure on the list of working class priorities. That is not to say don't include them, but the priority order might need revisiting. The language certainly needs revisiting. The framing needs revisiting – how do each of the issues we cover sound when we frame them in working class terms, taking account of the realities of working class life? If we are focus-grouping policies and manifestos and democracy reviews, have we gathered as many working class activists together as possible to help shape the messaging and ensure they are contextual and relevant? Could we consider a paid team to lead on this whole area, as the paid work seems to gravitate towards members that are not financially struggling to begin with? It might be interesting to break up the echo chamber effect and is one positive way of modelling as an organisation what kinds of knowledge and skills we truly value in helping to shape our work as a party going forward. Not just talking about "healing rifts" with our heartlands, but investing in it and demonstrating we are serious.

A party of radical social action, which is what we could and should be, should not be relying on over-stretched middle class members to "go out into communities" led usually by paid middle class "Community Organisers" to show poor people that they care about food banks and strikes. This is great, but social action within our party could meaningfully extend to actually employing more working class people. Auditing how many people from lower socio-economic backgrounds are able to access things like paid positions, senior positions and political candidates courses, what mentoring we are setting in motion and then reporting back to the membership on this.

We do need to win and we can't do that without strengthening and healing our connection with our own working class. We don't deserve to win if we continue to neglect that. The youth vote is on our side, but it is doubtful there will be sufficient numbers of woke students to enable us to achieve a win if we have yet again talked the talk on "taking power to all sections of society" and democracy to the membership but then just left the working class yet again as bystanders to power, cast as the recipients of benevolent party goodwill, the Alt Right and the likes of Cummings and Johnson waiting in the wings, Heil at the ready. Who even knows if we will still have a BBC by the next General Election? We could launch our own podcast or news channel, reporting on the impacts of various news items on working class life. Hell, we could even recruit some working class activists to present it.

To MPs trading on the catch-all terminology "Working People" – including our union chiefs – not only will your linguistic fudge do nothing to repair working class alienation from Labour and from left politics, which has now effectively become a gigantic middle class echo chamber, it risks actively further alienating the very people we need to show respect to. We see you, when you do this, so please think about the words you use. "Working class" describes a proud history of collectively fighting bosses and management to get a fairer deal for those of us without the clout of social status to trade on for a decent wage and standard of living. "Working people" doesn't. Boris Johnson is a "working person". "Working Class" means serially trashed by de-industrialisation and now by austerity and almost total political invisibility, to the point where forced to vote for actual class enemies in order to be heard. "Working People" doesn't.

The sleight of linguistic hand is a cheap trick which foolishly assumes a stupidity that has now been shown beyond doubt to not exist. Politically uneducated we may be, but stupid we are not. Linguistic tricks enable politicians to sidestep the issue, whilst appearing to care and whilst enabling middle class activists to claim we are all in the same boat, but in these key senses, that is just not the lived reality. If it was, the "Red Wall" would not have fallen in the dramatic way it did. Plus linguistically sidestepping an issue doesn't make it go away. It's an embarrassment to Socialism. Just stop it.

We may have swapped cloth caps and whippets for call centre headsets and tracker devices, but social class division is as rife as ever. The patterns and nature of how those power divisions are maintained are fairly stubborn and academically well-documented. It should be unacceptable to minimise this or hijack this very real issue by shifting it onto other strands of inequality, because they have protection. Something is being done about them.

The middle class left, through Corbyn's Labour, have effectively bestowed a selective policies that would over time alleviate (not reverse) inequality and the worst effects of austerity, which fell on our communities primarily, without giving the working class their say and without shifting the balance of power in any significant way.

The manifesto didn't reflect the absolute wholesale tarnishing and crushing of the working class in this country. Some of us are sick to death of these abuses and the tumbleweed of comment on them from within our party. With the cleansing of working class voices from Labour Party politics and of working class communities from our gentrifying cities, the cultural normalisation of demonising and denigration of working class people through vile TV shows, the absence of working class writers and actors from our screens and the middle class' abject failure to recognise talent when it speaks to them in the wrong accent or with a bit too much fire, we are now the second worst nation behind only Russia for public lack of trust in politics and business.

Someone I persuaded to join the party, who had long since lost interest in Labour, after a few months of membership, recently described us as now being a "Middle Class Joke". I have put my children and life on hold attending hundreds of meetings and sacrificed a functioning right hip canvassing, to retain Corbyn and try to get him into Number 10. I have nothing but admiration for him, but I have to admit, it's been too fluffy, too distant from the hard realities of working class life and concerns here in this country and EU referendum divisions aside, we messed this up.

We have had a desert of Socialism in British politics for so long that Corbynism provided the oasis, but for me it is just the start. We need to address working class absence and rejection as we would any other under-represented group subject to unconscious (and sometimes overt) discrimination. We need to own our prejudices and apologise properly. Once would be enough. Then we need to be seen to be finally taking this seriously and we need to do this without delay.

Those of us privileged enough to care and be able to speak out on Palestine and other issues should crack on but we need to be at least as vocal about issues of social injustice at home, because people – almost always working class people – are dying and living miserably here too. As activists and in conference we mention it, but no one spends hours debating why that is and why those power structures appear to be replicated and rife even within our own party.

There's a whole raft of science telling us why that happens but we're just not interested enough to even talk about it. We could change it if we did. As my armed forces veterans and families activist friend says "We are very limited in what we can actually do about Palestine right now". We need to get into government and most people aren't endlessly debating the issues we are. We need to focus on what we can change and what's relevant to the people we need to win back, here and now. Unite the Union set and missed their targets on class inclusion but at least they set some.

It's been fun repeatedly chanting at rallies and kidding ourselves that the middle class army alone can swing this. To say that didn't work would be an understatement. It's time to emerge from the bubble and start being real Socialists. If we want working class Labour voters to come home, we need to make sure we give them a decent one to come back to.

Why You Should Care About the Conservative Party

Phil Burton-Cartledge @philbc3

"Far left ideologue". Lecturer in Sociology at the University of Derby. Contributor to Tribune, Jacobin, *and* Politics, Theory, Other *plus several mainstream publications and outlets.*

Blog: All That Is Solid

Joined Twitter 2009
10,700 Followers

I am writing a book about the decline of the Tories. Yes, really.

At the time of writing, the Conservative Party have been in power for 44 of the last 75 years, and were returned with an 80-strong majority at the 2019 General Election. We also know when the Tories are in office what that means for our people. In the last decade, it has meant an increase in premature deaths, a backward slide in UK life expectancy, schools and hospitals starved of cash, and minority ethnicities targeted by hostile environment policies and scapegoated for Tory failings. For those who the Tories look after, the rich, life is tickety-boo. The food bank queues grow, but the share of national income taken by the wealthiest fifth of the population has grown to 40%. By contrast, the poorest fifth of the population make do with just 8% of the UK's income. These figures, highlighted on the website of the campaigning Equality Trust, are derived from the Office for National Statistics' survey of the 2017-2018 financial year.

We know what the Tories stand for, what they do, and why they do it. And that, surely, is all we need to know? For Socialists in the Labour Party, and the left outside of it, our concerns have to be about mobilising people and encouraging them into oppositional political activity, and our collective coverage of the Tories reflects this. It tends to be about the latest outrage they're pushing through or how certain Tory politicians stand to gain thanks to shares in, or some sort of relationship with, businesses profiting from the privatisation of this, or the contracting out of that. This is certainly a step above the tittle-tattle of who is-shafting-who that obsesses mainstream politics commentary, but not much. The sad truth of the matter is the left do not take the Tories seriously enough, and that is one reason (though by no means the only reason) why they keep winning.

What do I mean by this? In the 1980s the late Stuart Hall produced *The Hard Road to Renewal*, an analysis of Margaret Thatcher that proved extremely influential. Drawing on the work of the Italian revolutionary, Antonio Gramsci, Hall realised while she was still in opposition that there was more to Thatcherism than simply another short-term Tory government. Thatcher was more than an office-seeking politician, she had a project for remoulding British society. In the context of a crisis in the state's political economy, her "authoritarian populism" combined hard law and order positioning with anti-immigration and borderline racist rhetoric. Then, as now, with their friends in the right wing press, Thatcher's Tories offered up a world of us vs them-ism, constructing a virtuous "we" against a non-white, semi-communist, semi-malingering, and semi-totalitarian Other.

While Thatcher promised to restore the authority of the state to smite the subversive enemies of Britain, Hall was worried the Tories might succeed in creating an alliance between sections of different classes on the basis of offering carrots alongside the stick. The Thatcherite pledge came with the Thatcherite promise of a popular capitalism and spreading prosperity. This was limited to freedom to buy one's council house, freedom from strikes and union bullies, freedom to be successful and own your own business. It was compelling for enough of the electorate to keep returning her governments despite an unenviable record of inner city unrest and industrial tumult. And it is a measure of Thatcher's success that the millions of property owners she helped create in the 1980s still pay the Tories electoral dividends well into the 21st century.

Meanwhile, facing down one section of the electorate while buying off another, Thatcher's programme of closing state-owned industries, creating vast private monopolies by selling off tax payer-owned assets like British Gas and British Telecom, and using North Sea oil revenues to fund tax cuts for the rich, what Thatcher was always about was the greater subordination of Britain to the blind whims of capital. In other words, like all Tories she was concerned with the enrichment of her class and the reproduction of the relationships sustaining their dominance and power.

Hall clearly understood what Thatcher was about, and you can see echoes of her "authoritarian populism" in Conservative Party electoral strategy still. From David Cameron to Theresa May and Boris Johnson, all have variously tried opposing an "authentic" people against elites and undeserving outsiders (in the latter case to an unwelcome and undeserving degree of success). For his part, Hall argued the left needed to be in the business of forging its own alliances, encompassing Labour, elements of the far left (the old Communist Party), workplace-based movements of workers and those in the "new" feminist, anti-racist, gay liberation and environmentalist movements. In other words, Hall argued the left needs to think matters through strategically via an understanding of the forces in play at any given time, an approach that fell on the deaf ears of successive Labour leaders who simply believed the route to electoral success was better marketing.

The old saying goes that you should never interrupt your opponent while they are making a mistake. That is true, but we have to know what they are doing first. Studying the Tories, looking at the tactical and strategic calculations behind their rhetorical emphases, policy initiatives, how they build their electoral coalitions and what they do to overcome their significant and persistent problems must be taken seriously. Not because analysing the Conservative Party is a fun exercise in and of itself, but because it is necessary from the point of view of building our own strategy to win. How can we take advantage of divisions in the ruling class and how they play out in their party if we don't keep an eye on them? How might the left identify sections of the electorate and those ripe for being mobilised against the Tories, if we don't pay attention to the contradictions of their support base? And how can we forestall their attempts at scapegoating vulnerable people if the left doesn't identify the contours of their strategies in advance?

Unfortunately, since Hall's contributions on "authoritarian populism", work of this character has largely fallen into neglect. If we are to stop the Tories in the 2020s and keep them out of power for good, we must scrutinise them, learn about them and from them, and work constantly to wrong-foot their schemes. You might not be interested in the Conservative Party, but they haven't won more elections and spent more time in power than any other party by being uninterested in us.

The Flame Lit by Corbyn Can Never Be Put Out

Chelley Ryan @chelleryn99

Yes I am the Michelle Ryan featured in Alex Nunn's book 'The Candidate'. Blogger & feature writer for the Morning Star.

Blog: turningthetideblog.wordpress.com

Joined Twitter 2013
28,200 Followers

Labour gained 3.5 million new votes in 2017 and won the biggest swing in vote share since 1945. Jeremy Corbyn's policies are the reason why – we must never forget this fact, or abandon the cause of Socialism. My tribute published by the Morning Star.

It seems appropriate somehow that it was on another April 4, 26 years ago, that I lost my precious dad to the ruthless cruelty of prostate cancer. At the age of 23, I was reminded that life is not fair, that bad things happen to good people.

Maybe that's why I'm not so shocked that on another April 4, we lose Jeremy Corbyn as Labour leader. And my feelings about it are not dissimilar to my feelings when I lost my dad too soon.

The anger I felt towards my dad's cancer for cutting him down in his prime, I feel towards all the forces that were waged against Corbyn's leadership to make sure he would never become Prime Minister, except more keenly because cancer doesn't have a brain. It is not conniving and selfish and devoid of compassion for the people it strikes down.

Encompassed in that group are the PLP, the Tory media and last but not least, the "People's Vote" lobby who bore relentless pressure on Labour to adopt a policy I knew – and I suspect many of them knew – would cost us a General Election.

But in the same way I felt anger towards my dad when I found out he'd been ignoring the early warning signs of his cancer, Corbyn does not escape my anger. He made mistakes. He should have stood stronger against those forces.

92

He should, even now, be speaking out against them.

In a recent interview he blamed Labour's 2019 defeat solely on the media. No mention of MPs who worked consistently to destroy him, or MPs who pushed for the party to become a Remain party, a stance that was electorally toxic and cost us our Red Wall seats.

Having said all that, Corbyn has been a truly wonderful leader. He's been strong against unbearable pressure, dignified against the most vile of personal attacks, principled, inspiring and loyal. For no-one can argue that Corbyn is not unerringly loyal.

When the PLP were bearing down on him trying to force his resignation in 2016, he refused to budge. His loyalty towards the members outweighed any amount of pressure he felt to stand down. And I'm so glad he stayed. Jeremy Corbyn has been a breath of fresh air blowing around what had become a moribund political scene.

The past five years have been exhausting, exhilarating and frustrating, but one thing they have not been is business as usual.

If I genuinely believed Liz Kendall, Yvette Cooper or Andy Burnham would have won a majority in the 2017 or 2019 General Elections, I might feel differently about where we are now, but I don't.

Labour have been losing votes and seats since Blair. The closest we came to significantly turning that tide was in 2017 when we gained 3.5 million new votes and won the biggest swing in vote share since 1945.

Corbyn's detractors are busy trying to airbrush that inconvenient fact from history but we must never let that happen.

The biggest and most significant difference between 2017 and 2019 was our Brexit position, which was rightly viewed as a U-turn on the promise made to respect the referendum result in our 2017 manifesto. A betrayal of trust.

Pro-Remain MPs who refuse to accept this fact publicly know it privately, and are simply trying to dodge any blame for the result.

Unfortunately, huge swathes of the membership are doing the same, hence the support for Keir Starmer. If you refuse to acknowledge the damage wrought by our Brexit policy, you're left with two options, either blaming Corbyn for being too left wing and radical – or the media who attacked him for it.

Both amount to the same conclusion – we need a safe centrist leader the media can't vilify. The fact Miliband and Brown perfectly fit this mould but also failed to win general elections because they failed to inspire the electorate seems to have passed them by.

With Corbyn as leader, even the Tory narrative on austerity has changed. This is no coincidence.

Anyone who thinks the Tories would be spending a single extra penny on our NHS or police service with Kendall, Burnham or Cooper opposing them at the despatch box, is very much mistaken. Corbyn scared them. The 2017 General Election result scared them. They know we handed them an easy win in 2019, giving their "Get Brexit Done" motto a power they didn't have in 2017, but they can't count on Brexit dividing the electorate in the next election.

All they can count on now is us going back to being Tory-lite, so our voters stay at home in enough numbers for them to win again.

And that's why I urge the members to stand strong at this time of change. We are Corbyn's legacy in the same way the values passed down to me are my dad's.

I might not agree with the majority of members on the reasons we lost the last General Election so devastatingly. I might believe the membership needs to better reflect our working-class voters, but I do agree with the majority of members who want to offer the electorate policies that will dramatically improve their lives and those of their loved ones.

Corbyn brought us together and we need to carry on holding the torch he lit together into the future, making it hard for any future leader to ditch a manifesto that is truly worth getting out to vote for.

If I'd had a look into a crystal ball five years ago and seen the way things would end, I would still have started the petition calling for an anti-austerity candidate to stand for Labour leader, I'd still have devoted my life to fighting for Corbyn to win that first leadership and the second and to protecting his leadership over the next few years.

I still believe the rock we have thrown into the stale political pond will be sending out ripples that will change political history forever and for the better.

Once the flame of hope is ignited, it is almost impossible to put out, especially if we guard against it.

So thank you Corbyn for lighting that hope in our hearts. We will never forget all you did for us. All our gains from now on will be made because of you.

Our Time Will Come: Corbyn and Sanders Are Bigger Than Electoral Politics

Rob Jones @robjonesdotuk

Hip Hop head, West Ham fan
Trustee for Crossroads Care East Sussex, Brighton & Hove
Branch Executive Committee Member for Brighton Queens Park
Labour Party

Blog: robjones.uk

Joined Twitter 2016
200 Followers

A Blog post from April 2020, looking at the positive legacy of two great Socialists.

It's incredible to be writing this knowing that Bernie Sanders has effectively dropped out of the race for the Democrat presidential nomination. Early in the race it seemed nailed on that he would win, giving the left a rare piece of hope for a better world.

Somehow, with a little help from his friends, Joe Biden managed to reverse the momentum to the point that Bernie couldn't see a way of winning, and so has suspended his campaign.

Pete Buttigieg, Mike Bloomberg, Amy Klobuchar, Andrew Yang and Tulsi Gabbard have all given their support to Joe Biden since dropping out of the race themselves. Only Elizabeth Warren seems interested in holding Biden to account now he's the presumptive nominee. Trump even thanked Elizabeth Warren for causing Bernie's ultimate defeat, implying that she stayed in the race long enough to split Bernie's support.

All this shows one thing – the Democrats remain as divided between the left and the centre of the party today as they were in 2016. When faced with a choice between the two, the party always seems to prefer the perceived safe option of a centrist candidate.

This isn't too dissimilar from the situation in the UK with the Labour Party. Jeremy Corbyn's leadership has been stained by smears from those within the party as well as outside of it, with both the

Parliamentary Labour Party as well as some of the member base perceiving him as unelectable, despite the popularity of what he stands for. Under Jeremy Corbyn, Labour became the largest political party in Europe. Unfortunately, that still wasn't enough to unite the two sides of the party for a common good.

With Keir Starmer's election as Labour's new leader, much like Joe Biden, he has replaced the radical left of the party with the moderate centre-left in the pursuit of power and the name of electability.

Both Corbyn and Sanders may be down and out, with both toppled by centrist forces in their own parties, but that doesn't mean their politics are.

It's long been a feature of UK politics that the older the voter, the more likely they are to vote Conservative. Interestingly, this time round that split seemed to exist within the Labour Party too. The younger the voter, the more likely they were to have been loyal to Corbyn.

The same split can be observed in the US. Both four years ago and now, there's a younger generation listening to Bernie's policies and ideas, and seeing that a brighter future can be achieved if we're brave enough to work towards it.

For a candidate like Bernie Sanders to challenge so convincingly for the nomination of the Democrats twice in a row, and four years apart, while appealing more to the youngest voters than to the oldest, suggests that his US brand of Socialism might not be as impossible a dream as it's seemed throughout history. While he stopped short of Corbyn's manifesto to nationalise broadband, railways and the postal service, he shared the core belief system that things like healthcare and education should be free to all as a condition of living in a developed country.

But why are these measures to promote equality more important to the younger generation now?

Firstly, young people in the UK, as well as the US, are significantly worse-off financially than their parents and grandparents were at the same age. Houses are relatively more expensive, causing a generation of renters who can only dream of affording their own home. That's if they're lucky enough to even afford rent in a world where precarious employment and zero-hours contracts are the norm, and where most opportunities to develop a career involve working for free at the beginning of it, which prices a lot of them out of following their hopes and dreams.

Many can't even afford to go to university to get the education that they need to force themselves away from these problems because the fees have risen so dramatically in recent history. A student going to university in the UK in 2012 would have paid triple what their older siblings did, and as a result, will also have accumulated 20% more debt than their parents would've at the same age. In the UK and the US, most younger people will never earn more in their lifetimes than their parents did.

This is the first time in history where that's a likelihood.

When the system has failed you, and when the future looks worse than the past, it's common sense to look for an alternative. Issues that are more prominent to the younger voters aren't addressed by anyone else. Housing inequality, stagnant and unfair employment and even sharply rising tuition fees simply don't matter for the Conservatives. They, and their voters, have already benefited from an unjust system and there's no rush for them to change something that suits them just fine.

When you've benefited from inequality, equality can seem just as bad. Let no-one tell you that overcoming that to change public perception will be easy, but I believe that the movements personified by Corbyn and Sanders are long from over, as are the struggles of the younger generation that have supported them. These inequalities have always existed, but they've never been part of the mainstream debate until now. As Corbyn and Sanders take their final bows, while these two politicians may have been rejected, the ideals and the politics they stood for haven't been. The fairer societies that they both called for will continue to inspire and inform political debate so long as the younger generations that they engaged continue to believe in their messages, and our time will come.

History Will be Very Kind to Jeremy Corbyn

Rick Evans @Skybluerick1

Reflections upon the enormous influence of Corbyn, originally written for my "changewemustobservationsfromtheleft" *Blog.*

As I write this we are in a Global Emergency because of Coronavirus and life is anything but normal at the moment. But we have now come to the end of Jeremy Corbyn's leadership of the Labour Party and I think that fact has been slightly lost somewhat in everything that's going on. There has been many people who have been vehemently against him being leader since he even won the leadership Election, I'm not one of those people that will be obvious to anyone who has ever read anything by me. So I wanted to write a thank you to Jeremy the most maligned person in British politics.

When the books in the future are written on this period in British history I believe they will be very kind to Jeremy Corbyn unlike so many during the last 5 years. He certainly was an unlikely leader and I think it's fair to say nobody expected it probably least of all himself. But the fact that he became leader against all the odds and energised and re-engaged so many in politics is a testimony to him and his vision of a fairer more equal society. The fact that so many in our own party never got him or his vision says more about them than him.

It's been said before but Jeremy is a different kind of politician entirely to the norm. Even compared to someone like John McDonnell who has similar views he's very different and that is something else I think that attracted so many to him. He has never been in politics for himself or for a glittering career but to actually help people and the struggles we all go through. Of course he's not the only one but so often in my lifetime at least it seems so many politicians weren't in it for the right reasons and over the years many people have become cynical, understandably, about them. This is one reason I believe some of his colleagues were never happy with him as leader as he was never part of the cosy House of Commons club.

Jeremy Corbyn grew up in a different political time in the 1960s and 1970s and was always firmly on the left. He cut his teeth as a NUPE union official and as a Councillor in Haringey when he was elected in 1974. At the time the Labour left were on the rise and in 1983 he was elected Labour MP for Islington North where he is still the MP. But as we know through the rest of the 1980s and 1990s the Labour Party lost Elections. While other left wingers shifted their positions on many things as the tide turned rightwards in a desperate attempt to get elected Jeremy stayed firm and always true to his beliefs. He carried on with all the causes he was involved with like the Campaign for Nuclear Disarmament, the Anti Apartheid Movement, Palestinian Rights and later the Stop the War Coalition.

Jeremy has consistently supported strikes and workers' struggles throughout his political life one of the few Labour MPs to do so. But by the time of the Blair years he was looked on as a dinosaur by some and was an irritation to the Labour government. He defied the whip 428 times while Labour was in power which has always been thrown back in his face and as used an excuse to criticise him. The difference through is when Corbyn criticised the New Labour government it was out of principle when so many criticised him it was to try to create an opportunity to get rid of him as leader. That's the blatant truth of it never has been someone been so bullied, betrayed, ridiculed and undermined yet he has always kept his dignity throughout unlike his opponents.

It's important to remember what had happened before Jeremy became leader because it's the events of the previous years that indeed lead to the tide of hope that got him elected as leader. To many including myself the New Labour governments of 1997-2010 had been a massive let-down and missed opportunity. Yes they did some good things like bring in the National Minimum Wage for example but especially post-Iraq many became cynical of Blair and didn't trust him anymore. Economically New Labour pretty much kept to the Neoliberal consensus of the Thatcher / Major years This laid the groundwork for the eventual surge of Corbyn and the rise of the new left. Older generations had always been told that we would have 'jam' tomorrow but New Labour didn't even promise us that. We were told that even at a time of economic success that in effect life in the late 1990s / early 2000s was as good as it was going to get. This coupled with the fact that our vote seemed to be taken for granted did New Labour no favours whatsoever.

This is why when Jeremy Corbyn spoke of hope and the end of Austerity he caught the mood of the young and Socialists who had all but given up. So many had grown tired of the soundbites and cynical behaviour of people like Alastair Campbell and Peter

Mandelson who didn't seem to have principles but rather just wanted to exercise power for power's sake. Corbyn sounded completely different to them and even though he had been around a long time it was very refreshing to some people who were unaware of him. It's often been said when Corbyn first stood for the leadership in 2015 that he was one of the nicest people in politics but that changed very quickly when it became obvious he was going to do well.

So it was during the first leadership Election that the knifes started coming out for him and that continued for the full course of his leadership only increasing in intensity. No matter how you look at it that made things more difficult for us and while it's true the majority of the press have always been pro-Conservative anti-Labour the attacks against Corbyn were on another level. The reason for that was very simple, it's because he is a democratic Socialist. The establishment were terrified of what he represented which is why the relentless smears carried on and on.

Although I've always been happy to call myself a Corbynist I prefer the term democratic Socialist because that is what will always last and at the end of the day what we will always be called. So in the same way the Bevanites or Bennites were Socialists so are the Corbynists it's just different eras. To me this was never about one man but a movement that was built around a modern Socialism. That's why I never got it when people went on about the cult of Jeremy or magic grandpa they were just silly smears to me. The people who said these things never got what it was about. Jeremy was the spark but so many things were happening with a left that had already been building up during the previous years but not in a conventional party political way.

That's why so many were surprised at the turn of events in the Summer of 2015. But the had been clues the previous few years with the rise of anti-austerity groups like UK Uncut. So what happened when Corbyn announced he was standing for leader was that he not only galvanised the traditional Labour left but the young and others involved in other campaigning. The coming together of that and the Corbyn surge was the most exciting thing politically I've ever felt a part of. To know that after years of being told that my views were out of date and from the past that so many had similar views was a brilliant uplifting experience that's hard to put into words. Similarly when Jeremy won the leadership on

September 12 2015 with 59.5% of the vote it's something I and many others will never ever forget.

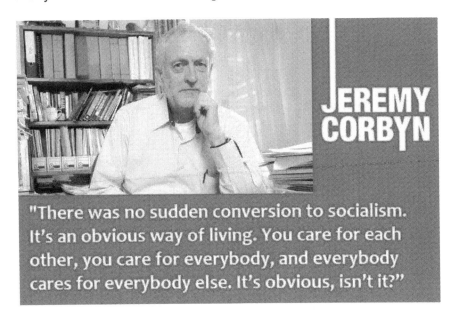

"There was no sudden conversion to socialism. It's an obvious way of living. You care for each other, you care for everybody, and everybody cares for everybody else. It's obvious, isn't it?"

So since Jeremy became leader it's been one battle after another having to defend him when we should have been attacking the Tories. The backstabbers have relentlessly attacked him instead of the Tories and I will never forgive them. During the Chicken Coup they actually tried to break Jeremy as a person that's what their intention was which was absolutely despicable. Those core MPs (we know who they are) who have spread the poison all along blame Corbyn for our election defeats and yet will take no responsibility themselves for making us look divided with their constant attacks on him.

Our Election defeats in 2017 and 2019 were a massive missed opportunity to start building a better society for all. Jeremy would have broken the rulebook and been a very different kind of Prime Minister. That would have been a fantastic thing and I could still cry when I think how even after all the relentless attacks on him by the media we were so so very close to winning in 2017. The backstabbers never understood that, they were expecting the 2019 result in 2017 because they are out of touch with a great swathe of people and it was our Brexit position which destroyed us in 2019.

So I want to thank Jeremy Corbyn for everything he has done for the party and movement. You helped so many believe that a different fairer type of society was actually possible after so many years of so many of us feeling hopeless for the future. He really is a unique politician. What he and his family have had to go through has been disgusting and I would have understood if he had quit as leader 4 years ago. But he didn't because he's made of stern stuff and he knew we were all behind him backing him. He helped bring a movement together and our challenge now is to keep that going. I'm glad he's staying as an MP and would like him to carry on doing that as long as he can. All the best Jeremy for the future and thank you. You brought hope back into politics and life itself and that will be your legacy.

We Are Corbyn: Self and Other, Politics and Political Activism

Gayle Letherby @gletherby

Sociologist, feminist, #Socialist.
Academic, civil celebrant, volunteer, activist.
Writer: research, fiction, memoir, political citizen journalism

Blog: Arwenack Creatives

Joined Twitter 2013
18,200 Followers

An assessment of Corbyn's Socialism, from my perspective as a sociologist and activist.

In his hugely influential, and still relevant, book *The Sociological Imagination* (published in 1959), the America sociologist Charles Wright Mills argued "neither the life of an individual nor the history of a society can be understood without understanding both".

Mills encouraged sociologists, and others, to look at the familiar and to see it afresh; to rethink the "things we take for granted" and "the things that everybody knows".

Part of this included a focus on the relationship between "personal problems" and "public and political issues" in that what is often presented as a personal responsibility or "failing" is in fact of public and political concern.

Just one example from Mills' analysis:

Consider unemployment. When, in a city of 100,000, only one man [forgive the sexist language Mills was writing 61 years ago] is unemployed, that is his personal trouble and for its relief we properly look to the character of the man, his skills, and his immediate opportunities. But when in a nation of 50 million employees, 15 million men are unemployed ... the correct statement of the problem and the range of possible solutions require us to consider the economic and political institutions of the society, and not merely the personal situation and character of a scatter of individuals.

For unemployment we might substitute homelessness, poverty, mental distress and so on. . . .

Mills was clear that sociologists had a political responsibility to understand the social world and to try to make it better. In recent years, some within the discipline have attempted to work with Mills' ideas and vision with a particular focus on the relationship between autobiography and biography (Auto/Biography) to further explore people's life experience. Through research and critical auto/biographical reflection such work highlights the relationship between the self (as in I, myself) and the other (those close to us and others less so) whilst at the same time thinking about the auto/biographical with reference to history and place (society). The academic (and political) equivalent then of "no (wo)man is an island" and a clear acknowledgement that – as grassroots and academic feminists in particular have added to the debate – the "personal is political".

In April 2017, at the start of a General Election campaign, Jeremy Corbyn gave a speech that made me reflect on Mills' writing. Amongst other things the then Leader of the Opposition spoke of his own political history and the history of British politics more generally and of past and present inequalities and injustices. Near the beginning of his speech he said:

… something hangs in the air. It typically goes unspoken. It's the unheard story of why so many of us are scaling back our hopes and dreams in favour of just getting by. It's the reason why this country is unable to unleash its potential. Because as families, communities – entire regions – we are all being held back….Being held back means we can't provide the life that we want for ourselves and those closest to us. And it hurts. It makes people angry and worst of all resigned to the idea that nothing can be done about it. We end up blaming ourselves or each other. This is life in modern Conservative Britain.

Referencing his own motivation and history was, and is, unusual for Corbyn. He said:

And now for a sentence I've yet to utter in my political life. Enough about you, what about me. In the 34-years since I became a MP, I have been attacked for what I believe in. But it has not changed my core values – and sadly many of the problems we faced then are still with us. In 1983, I stood up in Parliament for the first time and used my maiden speech to condemn deeply damaging cuts in public services and the NHS. It's a tragedy that I could make a very similar speech today and it would once again hold true.

Corbyn has, and continues to be, the brunt of so much criticism and personal abuse it's a wonder to many how he manages to stay standing, let alone continue to work tirelessly for others, also spoke of the need to challenge leadership. He referred to his willingness to being criticised, when the case is reasoned. Lack of challenge, he suggested, can lead to poor decision making and to arrogance.

There was much positive response to Corbyn's speech. Many were moved and inspired by it. Below is an extract from Jeff Goulding's Blog, "Ramblings of an Ordinary Man". The post was entitled "Forged in the Fire of Protest: A Prime Minister for the Many":

In an epic journey from Trade Union organiser to Labour Councillor and from the backbenches of Parliament to leader of a movement of more than half a million people and growing…

His rise to prominence and passionate defence of the weak and the disadvantaged has seen him vilified and abused, both personally and politically. In all that he has never wavered not even for a moment. His principles and values remain as strong today as they were forty years ago. Is this not the definition of strong and stable leadership? . . . .

As I write this I am conscious that it is laden with emotion. I have deleted and then retyped sentences, striving to be more analytical, objective and unbiased. But why should I be. I have tears in my eyes as I pen this, precisely because I am moved by the vision set out today by Jeremy Corbyn for the country and for the style of leadership he offers us.

Although often reluctant to speak of himself Corbyn has never been shy, in his lifelong quest for equality and social justice, of highlighting how the life chances and experiences of others is shaped by the intersection of biography, history and society. Although initially subject to much ridicule, and until the end of his time as LOTO often shouted down by those on the government benches, and sometimes shockingly by those behind him, his inclusion of the personal experiences of teachers, mothers, carers, Universal Credit applicants and so on powerfully highlighted how 'personal problems' ARE 'public and political issues.

So, what about me and how my own life experiences impact on my political identity and activism? In my mid 20s my (to my knowledge) one and only pregnancy ended in miscarriage at 16 weeks. Having worked as a nursery nurse but feeling unable to work with children at that time and finding part-time admin work unfulfilling I returned to education to study 'A' Level sociology. An undergraduate degree and doctoral studies followed which gave me the opportunity to engage in intellectual reflection on my own, and others, experience of miscarriage (undergraduate final year dissertation) and subsequent infertility and involuntary childlessness (PhD). From my own experiences I felt that pregnancy loss and non-motherhood were both misunderstood and under-researched and during my research I came across many others who felt the same. I met and talked and corresponded with women (and men) who had had experiences more distressing than mine; individuals whose reproductive "failures" dominated their lives completely. I also came across others for whom reproductive loss and non-parenthood was less significant or something that they felt they had "dealt with" and "left behind" the issue. Whatever their experience all spoke of how not achieving parenthood (or achieving parenthood in non-conventional ways) often marked them out as different, as other, and sometimes made them feel lesser.

Now self-defining as more (biologically) voluntarily childless than involuntarily childless I credit this personal shift in part to the opportunities my academic endeavours have given me for detailed reflection on my own experience and those of similar others. An opportunity, a privilege, that most people do not have. My friendships with younger people including the children and grandchildren of others is significant too as is my work – as teacher, supervisor, and mentor – in that all these relationships give me much opportunity for satisfaction and fulfilment. Of course I cannot know how my own life would have turned out if I had carried my baby successfully to term or if I had conceived and given birth to other children. I may have returned to education and study I may have not. I do know that this (and other) losses have significantly influenced by intellectual and personal development, opportunities and life experience.

My long-term interest in, and support for, the politics of the left was further stimulated in the Summer of 2016 (following the EU Referendum and the coup against the Labour Party leader). Inevitably my concern with and reflection on party politics was, and is, influenced by my feminist sociological interest in the personal as political *and* the political as personal. My status as non-mother is relevant too.

When five and a half years ago I stepped down from a full-time academic position (60+ hours a week being usual) to work freelance I was able to spend more time in voluntary activities and political activism. From 2016 onwards I quickly became active in canvassing, protesting on the street and online and in political writing (including letters to newspapers, writing for my Blog, and contributing to the social media presence of my CLP). I have written about school Summer holiday hunger, the Grenfell Tower tragedy, the Windrush generation, homelessness, health, education and more. I do appreciate that such involvement and activity might be more difficult, not least in terms of organisation as well as time, for friends with children and grandchildren.

The (small amount) of political work I do is motivated by my strong desire for a better world for all, now and in the future. Many of my concerns then are for all "our" children, their life chances and choices. With all this in mind I was disappointed (and hurt) for my *difference,* my *otherness* to be highlighted yet again when I read of the launch of "Mums4Corbyn" at "The World Transformed" event at the 2018 Labour Party Conference. From what I could see of planned events many of the issues considered were those that affect all women, mother or not, and shared concerns were part of my pitch for a piece for the *New Socialist* who published a series of articles focusing on the contemporary politics of motherhood in support of the initiative. Thus:

My concern is with the political significance of all women whether mothers, non-mothers or other-mothers (women whose mother status is considered lesser, even "unreal"). This is important because the ideologies and expectations of ideal motherhood affect all women, in our private and our public lives and the image of the ideal woman – which is arguably synonymous with the image of the ideal mother – also affects us all, whether mother, other-mother or non-mother. Feminism can be criticised for focusing on motherhood at the expense of a consideration of sisterhood. Yet any (political) understanding of motherhood and mothering needs to embrace the experience of non-mothers and other-mothers. It is only through such holistic reflection on our similarities and our differences that as sisters together we can challenge that which divides us and holds us back and celebrate our "collective and communal relations" which will enable to us work together for "transformative change".

I appreciate, of course, the particular challenges and inequalities that mothers face but I maintain that we can more effectively work on this together as, in with reference to this issue, as in many others, we do indeed "have far more in common with each other than things that divide us" (Jo Cox MP).

Sadly, the editors felt that my piece did not "quite match" their intended agenda. Which in turn felt, to me, like a further denial of the relevance of the very many of us who have an identity and experiences often defined by society as lesser.

I include this personal example to highlight how even within an inclusive community one can feel *othered* and I suggest that it is important to be aware of and sympathetic to the differences between us. Not least when the community itself if subject to *othering*. Through social media networks, identified not least through hashtags such as #WeAreCorbyn, #GTTO, #SocialistSunday, #IStandWithDianeAbbott, #CorbynWasRight, and so on, and through my local CLP, "The World Transformed", Labour Assembly and other such initiatives I have made connections with, made friends with, a large number of like-minded political others. On Twitter and Facebook, during debate at the party's Annual Conference and at other fringe events I am often moved and empowered by the personal stories that people share. Stories of personal struggles and political awakenings, of community action and activism, of hope for the future, of passion and of care for others. Like so many others I remain inspired by and grateful to Jeremy Corbyn for everything he has done and continues to do. In the networks I have made we don't always agree but we do (almost always) respect and support each other.

As I wrote recently on Twitter (April 10 2020):

In July 2018 after being a few years on Twitter I had less than 800 followers, now mostly due to #Socialist friends I have just under 18,000. I enjoy the debate. I love the camaraderie. I am grateful for the support & for all I've learnt from all of you. The last few months have been hard for us. The # GE19 result was devastating, the attacks on Jeremy Corbyn have continued & the election and the first few days of Keir Starmer as LOTO more than disappointing. Lots of members have left / are leaving the party. Others, myself included, have argued for staying: to fight from within. I appreciate the pros and cons of both decisions so no pitch here (I can't promise not to make my points in other Tweets though!). But, whether inside OR out of UK Labour we represent something HUGE: an interested, engaged, active social movement. Hundreds of 1000s of folk fighting for equality, social justice & a safer more sustainable world #4TheMany No one can deny that & we mustn't give it up. IN or OUT we really are #StrongerTogether #Solidarity

Such support is invaluable when abuse and attacks not only of Jeremy Corbyn but also of those of us who support him has become the norm. When as a group we are defined as other – here are some examples from my Tweets:

September 18 2018

On top of everything else I'm now apparently a "hard left boot girl" (Vince Cable) Actually: I'm a 59 year old white woman of working class origin. First in my family to go on to higher education (a polytechnic and proud of it) aged 28.

June 1 2019

It seems, in thinking the #Campbell expulsion from LAB was justified, I am a "posh boy Stalinist". As a 60 year old woman fighting for a better world #4TheMany I'm not sure whether to laugh or cry.

April 14 2020

Yesterday I had "the intelligence of a crayon", I am a "thick Labour bint" – for posting positive responses under Corbyn's tweets. What horrifies me is that such attacks are now the norm & that some folk clearly spend their days waiting to fling bile at JC/JC supporters.

I don't consider myself to be part of a cult. Neither do I think that I am deluded or stupid or any of the other things I and similar others have been called over the last nearly five years. What I do passionately believe, with reference to my own life experience to date – as a sometime carer and as someone who has needed professional (as patient) and personal (as daughter, wife, friend) care from others, as a student, a teacher, a researcher, a volunteer, a women and a citizen – is that Jeremy Corbyn's Labour was a once in a lifetime chance. In 2020 as we continue to lick our political wounds and reflect on *what next* a continued acknowledgment that "personal problems" are "public and political issues" and that critical reflection on the relationship between self and other as an essential part of our approach is, I think, the only way forward.

Keir Starmer's First Days as Labour Leader

Bob Miller @hctbn

An initial assessment of Starmer, posted as a Twitter thread.

OK – for those fed up with the new Labour leadership and thinking of leaving the party, here are my thoughts...

So far as the leader of the Labour Party that I would like to see goes, I would give Keir Starmer about two or three out of ten...

He committed to left policies, but it's too early to judge.

He committed to unify the party – I think he has a finely crafted Shadow Cabinet with a couple of nods to the left, but a few appointments specifically chosen to piss off the left and result in as many of the left leaving the party as possible.

His political performance as leader of the Labour Party has been decidedly wishy-washy. He has challenged the government on the Coronavirus exit strategy (the Achilles Heel of Blair and Bush's Iraq strategy).

But what about PPE for hospitals, GPs, and care workers, testing, care homes being used as de-facto hospices, availability of oxygen in hospitals, supply of food packages to at risk groups (including the ones excluded from the at risk list), accurate reporting of deaths (inside and outside of hospitals), financial support of those left out so far, etc, etc?

And that's before the lies we are continuously being told. Of course there are other aspects to British political life that should be being challenged – the Russia report, Priti Patel no-shows (and continued determination to exclude "low" skilled workers from the UK – you know, the ones keeping us alive), and much more...

But even a wishy-washy Labour government is infinitely better than the very best Tory government, and this is far, far below even an average Tory government. Even before coronavirus there were millions in poverty, suffering from the policies of this government (many of which were introduced in good faith by New Labour and then weaponised by the government of Cameron & co). There are people living in housing that is unfit for purpose, housing that is a clear and present fire risk, and they are the lucky ones they actually have a roof over their heads. There are people who have zero job security, jobs that do not pay enough to live on, with employers like Sports Direct or Wetherspoons, and there are many employers that are even worse.

So....

Am I happy with Starmer's first days as leader? No.

Do I trust Starmer? No (I may have mentioned that).

Will I be leaving the Labour Party? No (at least by my own volition).

Will I fight for left wing (I prefer to think of them as Socialist) policies? Yes.

Will I support a Labour Party led by Starmer to get a Labour government into power?

** HELL YES! **

Because people without a voice are relying on us to do what is right. And always remember....#NeverTrustATory.

Undeterred and Undefeated, Winter Turns to Spring

Mandy Clare @Mandy4Dene

Thoughts, written during April and May 2020, on the leaked internal Labour report about the disciplinary process, plus the politics of COVID lockdown.

"Undeterred and Undefeated, Winter Turns to Spring". Those words appear at the end of what was Tony Benn's favourite song, written by Robb Johnson, which I heard sung by him over Zoom for the first time recently.

When I first heard it I thought it referred to the left's ability to turn back the tide in the historical ebb and flow of cyclical power struggle between the left and right of the Labour Party. Looking at all that has happened within the broader context of recent events, I wonder now if those words might better describe a broader natural occurrence whereby the working class eventually don't wait any longer for the Labour left to regroup and learn the lessons. Maybe they just get sick of always coming last and never getting a proper say and take matters into their own hands.

Who has the energy to go through endless cycles like the last five year battle we have endured? In any case, time has already run out for all those killed by austerity, through avoidable virus contagion, and now yet again in the UK and the US, through being black and being working class. A dramatic tipping point seems to be fast approaching where party politics has exhausted its final chance to be the solution to the neglected problems faced by the voiceless. The working class seem to be leading on this one.

That Labour Report

So we have a new Labour leader and a pandemic. Just as we come to terms with these monumental events and try to adapt, as if that is even possible, the full colour version of something we had all seen unfolding, but been unable to prove over the period since Corbyn took office as leader, lands with an unceremonious thud, in the form of a leaked internal report on the handling of Anti-Semitism complaints.

Although we had heard some details of foul play, bullying or sabotage at the top, it is probably fair to say that reading this report has still left many of us absolutely reeling. We have all sympathised with Corbyn for the mauling he has endured on our behalf, often with next to no back-up from people who presented themselves publicly as having his and our backs. We talk less about the impact on us as members, as activists, as people with families and jobs and everyday worries and concerns to juggle, through all of this. I want to share with you some of my reflections on that because I think it is important. We can still hope and we can still win, but first we need a reality check and time to process and come back together.

When I first started supporting Corbyn and became active, many people said to me that no one – not the media nor the political establishment – would ever allow someone like Corbyn to succeed. Wanting them to be wrong, wanting nothing more exciting than basic human dignity and day to day security within a wealthy Western society, the daily turbulence and grief we on the left have had to endure is almost indescribable. There isn't a word for the daily lived trauma of feeling attacked and vilified, or of being made to feel that it is you that is causing disunity and making the party unelectable. Electability and unity have been the buzz words of the campaign and how many of our allies through the Corbyn leadership have bought into that following our painful and resounding defeat in December 2019?

Were we factional, or have we been serially gaslighted? Because from the information that has emerged and pending confirmation by the party of its validity, it very much looks like those using the arguments to drive us out are now using the same narrative to continue to control the left. If there is disunity and we don't get elected it must be the fault of the left. As shocking as this report is, it does at least present a potentially serious challenge, at last, to that unfaltering narrative targeted at the left.

As someone who once managed a domestic abuse project, I can tell you that gaslighting is a thing. Many, many abusive behaviours take place within a framework of gaslighting and it's worth taking five minutes to assess these revelations within that framework. The very purpose of gaslighting is to cause the victim to feel they are to blame and at fault and to play on their decency in a long drawn-out guilt trip. Success comes in the form of the victim becoming subdued, questioning themselves and their judgment or inherent decency, and wearing themselves into the ground with frustration and over-thinking until, none the wiser despite all of the self-analysis, they give up.

There is no way to emerge unscathed from gaslighting but your best chance of damage limitation is to cut all ties with the perpetrator, to go "no contact". Yet we on the left, through our commitment to the values we believe belong at the heart of the Labour Party, have been frozen in place, unable to leave. As with any dodgy relationship, part of the reluctance to simply call it quits is the feeling of having put in all that time and effort and it having been just wasted. It's hard to walk away and admit defeat but staying only damages the victim further.

Victims of systematic, prolonged abuse will tell you, it's confusing, exhausting, demoralising and fraught with self-blame and self-doubt. If you're feeling exhausted right now don't worry – you're not alone and it is a normal human response. It takes time to grieve properly and there is no short cut to getting straight in your head what has been done to you and how. Even when you do, sometimes there is never any resolution as to how people can sometimes behave the way they do, or why they would put so much energy into something so utterly destructive, when it could have been so good for everyone through some co-operation. The work of Kate Pickett and Richard Wilkinson on inequality outcomes shows clearly that inequality harms the health and wellbeing of everyone – not just those at the bottom – and that more equal societies are happier and healthier across the board. So that would also include any funders that may have vested interests in keeping things as they are. I'm just saying. It's not naive to fight for greater equality, it is in everyone's interests – even those of active saboteurs. And we came very close, despite everything cooked up behind closed doors to stop us. So we are not giving up. Whether inside or outside of this party and no matter what emerges from this investigation, we will not go away and we do not buy into the abusive gaslighting.

The mainstream media cacophony in support of this gaslighting created for us an even more densely toxic atmosphere in which to survive. It has been like seeing the unhinged word salad of your abuser reflected back at you from every screen and newspaper, every car radio news bulletin, multiple times every week or even daily, until you become the inevitable cliché, turning to your social media echo chamber for some reassurance that there is still something good in the world and something to hope for. Or maybe that was just me, but I'm sure we have all had our coping mechanisms if we have managed to stay in the party through this extraordinary time.

In a post-Jo Cox era of increasing verbal and online abuse against political representatives, myself and fellow Labour Councillors have been publicly labelled "Marxist Extremists" and worse by a local Conservative Councillor, on a community social media platform. This happened repeatedly, only stopping when I threatened to formally complain about their behaviour. Amidst the general swirl of hatred and misrepresentation, we on the left dug deep and sought reasons to carry on, some of us becoming elected as Councillors, fewer as MPs – part hope, part defiance spurring us on as we believed we were creating something bigger and that the end to this nonsense was in sight, especially after we came so close to winning in 2017. We could not stomach the prospect of losing in 2019, although the atmosphere across the media, amongst the party and particularly on the doorstep had really changed. It was a real slog – we convinced ourselves it was like the final stages of childbirth (possibly just me again).

With hundreds, maybe thousands, of door knocking hours under our belts, not only did we bomb, we were told it was our fault, by those who allegedly thwarted this party – and thwarted everyone who depended on our success, in order to have anything like a dignified and hopeful life – meticulously and joyfully, by those employed to get us over the line. There aren't words for the feeling in the pit of the stomach when that context comes to mind, when we recall the number of times we have been told as if we are naive children that it's all very well and good having wealth distribution on the agenda, but you can't do anything about it if you are not in power. Look us in the eye now and tell us again why we aren't in power to make those changes.

On behalf of the people that have died and are still dying, I would like to say that no, we aren't naive to care about that, or to have a determination to face daily abuse and undermining in order to do something about that. I don't need to spell out the potential implications of this leaked report and the apparent denial of electoral success for democracy at large. I know I am not alone in feeling mind-blown every time I try to wrap my head around the scale of it. Even though really, we knew....

Zooming in on the Issues

We have a Labour leader now who is a barrister, who campaigned that, being from a working class background, they have invested their time for free in the name of social justice throughout their career. This is great news, because he will be able to help us work out which part of the law covers electoral fraud if it turns out that the actions alleged within this internal report turn out to be true. He can help us to ensure that legislation is put in place to cover it, if there isn't any.

It hasn't been a barrel of laughs on the left within Labour these last few years. It felt too much of the time that a culture of entitlement and territorialism seemed to seep downward and penetrate almost every sphere of activity within the party. For me, nothing has been easy or felt right, as a result. We are socialists. Where is the respect? I would not have encouraged anyone in the end – particularly if they were also dealing with pressures of low income – to become involved in the hierarchy side of things (or at least not without a health warning). If being a Corbyn supporter has been arduous, being a working class leftie has at times felt like having a tattoo on your forehead. Having said that, I have made close friendships as a result of sticking around. What an amazing network we are.

I can't speak for anyone else. I imagine others feel similarly winded. Because of lockdown I have attended a few Zoom meetings and presentations. People on the left are reaching out to each other, there seems to be a sense of disarray and confusion with no roadmap to follow in order to pick ourselves back up. It's so strange to think that all those "World Transformed" and Conference fringe sessions turn out to have been fairly pointless, not to mention costly. What began as a bright spark of hope for a new politics seemed to morph into a series of vanity showcases, focussed on a fairly narrow range of pet recurring obsessions. It never felt robustly left. It was lacking in older people who could share the cyclical history of left and right within the party and devoid of working class voices of all ages. You can look at the sum total of what we have achieved after that epic left / right battle reprise that we didn't really start, other than by just existing and either see a bleak horizon or something to build on; lessons learned. Like everyone else I am still working it out. So are my friends.

Some thoughts from these lockdown Zoom sessions with respected comrades and with good friends are helping us to process and begin to fathom what might need to come next, so I would like to share some of these with readers in case they are helpful. Some are mine and some are from other people. We seem to be broadly concluding the same sorts of things:

1. We haven't had it in us to treat people as we have been treated. Regardless of our distaste with many of Blair's policies and decisions the left didn't have it in them to dismantle the party to try to get their own way. Politics is dirty. We probably need to toughen up and perhaps anger can be our ally. We should never stop being vocal and fighting for what we believe in – whether inside or outside Labour.

2. Many activists joined because they trusted Corbyn's authenticity and wanted to do something good. That is wonderful, but it's not enough to be engaged on the left politically just because we have a moral sense of kindness and want to do good things. This is not a charity. It is more about justice than kindness. Systems of oppression work in certain predictable and stubborn ways and we need to understand those systems of control much better in order to be effective. We need to be able to dismantle the rhetoric of social mobility in order to fight for social justice because there is a world of difference between the two. We failed as a movement to put in place decent quality, accessible, political education that would empower members to critically evaluate and work out the most effective approach. This needs to go deeper than a cursory knowledge of Marx. It needs to move beyond training sessions on how to effectively door-knock and canvass, to include established critical analyses of what the inherent flaws are within party politics as a vehicle for meaningful shifts in who holds power. We need to take time to really understand how and why the left tends to fail, as many of these patterns are not new. It can be done in fun ways and quite quickly, but is going to require us to have dialogue with each other on identified works and themes to understand them better and be more skilled, determined and unified in understanding and articulating our position.

3. Did we properly get to grips with an understanding of where the real decision-makers and king-makers reside, not just within the organisational structures of the party but also, possibly more so, within the biggest unions? If we are masochistic enough to stick around, we need to collectively navigate these. This is vitally

important because the unions themselves are not model democracies and are absolutely alien to many within Labour, never mind the wider working class, for whom they were once a trusted source of back-up and support at work. Crucially, they were a natural hub for development of class and political consciousness and importantly, a route for those closed out of having a political voice into cultivating and platforming their own. This is important because the public – especially the working class public – are attuned to a good socialist message delivered in their own language by someone who comes across as passionate and genuine. We need the working class voice within the top tiers of our party as much as the working class need a Labour Party that gets them. We also need to make connections with and offer support to some of the emerging new unions that are managing to win back the support of the working class.

4. The working class left and those with left sympathies need to be made to feel they have a place and that their voice, and how they articulate their lived experience of political issues, is valid and welcome. Too often, straight talking has been rejected or re-framed as aggression, for example. The working class, whether they are aware of this or not, have the highest stake in the left succeeding within the party structures, but by our neglect of them, by our not even noticing the extent to which middle class activists squeeze them out, discredit and even bully them into silence, even when they can be bothered to keep trying, we have left an open political goal for the opposition and worse, for Fascism. The answer to this cannot lie in "here is what we are trying to do for you" or "we're on your side, you idiots" sentiments, or in handing out food parcels. We have to work now to identify concrete and creative ways that we can re-embed left politics and fire within working class communities. Again, we do this by taking our lead from working class people. We also do this by making political education sessions relevant and accessible in as many different engaging formats as possible. There are left ex-services veterans, low income single parents and others within the party that are willing to reach out, and ideally placed to dialogue with working class people who have shifted to the far right, away from Labour. We are not resourcing that. It should be a top priority. All of this political education activity should be a regular staple of left activism that we share across our networks, not a tacked on extra that happens once in a red moon. It is not meaningful left activism without this. We should fight for funding from the unions and other organisations, for budgets to develop this work properly.

5. Our CLP and other meetings need to be actually political, with plenty of time given to critical analysis of the economic and political systems and the party and unions themselves. They should not be sterile environments that function to do everything except meaningful analysis. These need to be linked to whatever challenges are showing up for the community locally. Through what structures can we band together to make the case and challenge where change is needed? How can we innovate and present things in outspoken and clear ways that show that we care but also show how that issue is a political and Socialist one? Quieter voices need to be drawn out and supported. We may need to encourage an etiquette where privileged people might be willing to step aside to make space for less privileged people to speak and take up formal positions. Everyone needs to respect that those seemingly doing heroic amounts of work may be freer to do so through relative privilege. Which brings me to the next point.

6. Celebrity left heroes. This has been disastrous in some ways. Activists have become so wrapped up in the buzz surrounding the elevated glitterati of the left, attending rallies and door knocks for the feel-good, that this has taken the place of the kinds of meaningful analysis and creation of support structures that, had we made time for them, might have yielded us a socio-economically diverse and fired-up PLP, to shake up the stale political universe we seem to have now very quickly reverted to. If we elevate some special people over others and put them on every platform going, of course they will become adept at public speaking and rabble-rousing. It might be more interesting to provide platforms for people who have traversed a greater social distance in order to be able to share what they know and what they see as important. The over-excited worship of celebrity and hierarchy doesn't really fit within a Socialist model – some might say that it is anathema and what we are wanting to get away from! At the end of the day, in a puff of glitter, our movement has all but vanished and we have to question whether we allowed ourselves to be distracted and deluded about how much progress we had actually made by enabling all of that hype – fun as it was.

7. Older activists can bring a grounded insight in lessons of the political past that younger graduate activists don't yet have, despite perhaps a wealth of book-learned Socialism from university and, if middle class, buckets full of confidence and things to say. Socialists of any age that have experienced prolonged low income living with

no end in sight have a lot to bring to the party. We cannot be ageist and Socialist.

8. No one particular left organisation has all the answers. All organisations have weaknesses and flaws. Frequently they detest each other. All of that is par for the course on the left. Wanting to control and dominate all other groups, whether in regard to local selections or slates, is more than just a flaw though, within a left and Socialist context. Perfect impartial democracy may not exist or may not deliver high calibre candidates able to do the job that we need and really inspire people to want to come with us on our journey, no matter what our policies. People need to trust and believe their candidates and trust in politics is very low in the UK. This is a problem that we need to come together to assess and fix. It isn't insurmountable, especially now that we have some breathing space due to the very weird combination of our abject failure to get elected into government and COVID-19 lockdown. We may need to fundraise for some kind of impartial online shared system. We may need to agree broad campaigns and actions we can join forces on without falling out, but no one organisation should be seeking to dominate in that process – if all organisations have an equal part to play, it dilutes the prospects of that. That any single organisation would seek to dominate is a bit questionable and should probably be regarded as distasteful and somewhat clueless, within a left context.

Some of us are leaving the party, some are staying in and some don't yet know. Of those leaving, some have left political activism for now or perhaps forever, to dig their garden or focus on their kids and just give themselves a break from the abuse and serial sense of loss and also, regrettably for some, of having been left open to attack and left un-defended. This is understandable and if people need to back off, they should.

Some have left and gone into other parties – these may or may not achieve either influencing the Labour Party's direction, may do well on their own terms or may fold. Some are staying in but engaging in broader ways, having taken their foot off the gas of winning CLP elections and vying for conference places. Given that we have all learned just how much of conference is actually in the hands of unions and not members, again, this is perfectly understandable. Some have decided that they will be very sparing with who they will canvass for in the future and again, although that will weaken the party overall, it is completely understandable. At the very least, I think everyone on the left deserves some time to rest up and reflect.

Some remain in the party with a determination (or weary resignation) to fight on. Of those, some are telling others that they too must stay in and fight. There are, as was discussed in a recent Zoom, good and well-rehearsed arguments on both sides – strong reasons for staying, strong reasons for leaving. I wouldn't like to say to anyone else what will be right for them or ultimately the right decision. For now, I think for me this is an interesting time. I did not like where we had been heading – it seemed an endless period of time that we had to silence ourselves whilst we watched decisions being made by those above us that seemed certain to lead to electoral disaster. It's also like an especially cruel form of torture to force people with strong social justice sentiments to keep their mouths shut for the sake of unity when they see power being abused.

Decisions were also made about how to handle hostile media and in-house attacks against members and the party's reputation that increasingly seemed to just further undermine the confidence and trust of those on the left who had given their all to put us in the best position to win. There seemed to be multiple incidences of special treatment of those in positions of power and privilege who were regularly and brazenly briefing the media and working against us and the party leader.

It's done. The inevitable has happened. There is some relief in that, like emerging from a bad relationship, because it feels like now we can begin the work within the left of putting ourselves back together stronger, wiser, tougher and to have the proper serious discourse and analysis – sans celebrities and glitter – that we have not somehow managed to ever properly have between dealing with crises and attacks.

We need to use this time now, this precious although painful, grieving pause, to do just that. Grieve, retreat if you need to, leave if you need to, but when you feel you can face it, engage with others. We can build something from this apparent theft. It may turn out to be something emerges within the party or it may become bigger than can be contained within the party. We should not underestimate what we have learned or can yet learn from each other.

Whatever it Takes

To say that the UK government have failed in their response to this virus would be an understatement, even before we look at the tens of thousands of excess deaths not formally attributed to COVID-19. Our new Labour leader is choosing to take a conciliatory and low key approach to opposition, although given the extent of government failure (second highest death rate in the whole world), hypocrisy (Cummings' trip to Durham), whitewashing their strategy (following the science, apart from when we don't) classist neglect (only those who can afford to keep their children home from schools can do so) and the care home carnage we seem to be well outside of the realm of criticising for criticising's sake.

These are just some of the illustrative examples of the magnitude of the failure which seems to present on the face of it nothing but malice and contempt for working class people by this government.

Piers Morgan suddenly discovering a moral compass and telling us we are being taken for mugs and shouldn't be standing for it is no comfort whatsoever. It just seems bizarre and suspicious and likely to be part of some other future attack on the working class in the making that we have not yet sussed out.

The government's contempt is exacted most viciously on anyone they feel cannot fight back, and they are good at honing in on and exploiting those vulnerabilities. It includes those who have taught, cared for and reassured our children and the vital staff – the cleaners and caterers – that have kept the schools open for vulnerable children and children of other frontline staff. As during other times of national threat and stress, the British spirit is alive and kicking, the problem is not the people but the extent to which we are disregarded and serially underestimated by those that we entrust with power, who really have no idea what it is like to live how we live.

Having said they would do whatever it takes to keep us all safe, people are now being sent back to work forcibly by government because that is what happens when you provide encouragement to business with no other financial alternative for their workers in a situation like this. Like a vulture circling for prey, they are starting on those who have the least political voice and power, those feeling pressurised by social duty and not letting down the team, or isolated in their fear by a lack of robust union support.

They are masters of this. Perhaps this explains Matt Hancock laughing in the face of a Sky News presenter doing her job in trying to hold him to account for strategic inconsistencies. They don't care. It must be hysterical to them that anyone could have believed otherwise.

The rest of us have already in effect sat back including many Labour Councils, including our new leader Keir Starmer and including unions and allowed that forcing of non-essential staff back to work to start to happen. In doing so, we allow the government to divide and conquer as they have so many times in the past. We are complicit in allowing this government to use working class children and families alongside teaching and other school staff as canaries in the mine, testing out with their own lives when it is safe for the rest of the population to emerge, whilst infection and death rates are still much higher than in other countries that have started to emerge from lockdown, and whilst the regional picture is far from stabilised. That is disgusting. It is a highly effective strategy of old that works brilliantly, but only if we let it.

What's Marx Got To Do With It?

What the protests in America, following the killing of George Floyd, seem to be showing us clearly is that people are sick of empty promises where the desperate need for justice is never satisfied. They are sick of divide and rule politics and all the same politics. The trust is gone.

Every time someone who is black or is working class appears on television to admonish those expressing the natural human anger felt at having been harmed by the institutions that are supposed to protect us, they are contributing directly towards bolstering this tried and tested divide and rule strategy. They are in effect contributing to more broken promises, more exploitation and more violence down the line. They are weakening the hand of the voiceless against those abusing their power and guilty of wilful neglect.

Anyone holding public office needs to remember where they come from and who they are supposed to represent. If they come from class privilege, then they need to be guarded against their tendency to fall in line against any oppressed group for an easier life or an easier climb to the top.

Working class people are not stupid. Most working class people can't quote you Marx, but still know that in a world where profit comes before everything else but doesn't come to us, we will be the first to be shoved back into the workplace to test out the conditions for everyone else. Great. We know that if another wave kills us and our immediate families, by-passing those furloughed at home because the government (divide and rule) can't risk alienating everyone to the same level or killing everyone all at once, which might raise an eyebrow even from Laura Kuenssburg, it will be deemed our own fault because some people went to the beach one day when it was sunny.

We too easily forget that it used to be possible and sane for a family to survive relatively well with only one parent having to work, and sometimes we don't clock that for middle class mothers, working is a choice and expression of feminism and personal expression, whereas for working class mothers, since the time of New Labour (helping the Tories out no end) it has been pretty much essential for survival and rarely fun or creative in any way. But all of these factors, along with the inevitable routine and increasing collapses of capitalism are detailed and predicted within Marx's work. So we as the exploited working class are not mugs, we know more than we think we do. Most people feel trapped and just want to survive and believe that things will work themselves out. It's tiring being exploited and always worrying about money. It's demoralising working in jobs where there is very little worker control or security and where we feel downtrodden, unheard and unvalued.

Managing Down Expectations

Is it possible that the working class now hate what they regard as the politically bland metropolitan and culturally sterile Labour party that they see as unable or unwilling to respect even their democratic vote even more than they detest the Tories? It was said to me more than once on the doorstep that people knew what to expect with the Tories. They expected the worst from them but were outraged beyond belief that Labour had worked to thwart democracy on the Brexit outcome.

Within our culture, profit comes before quality jobs but many of our kids have never known what having a quality job feels like. It comes before the wellbeing of our alienated downtrodden working class communities and also before the political and business elite's Darwinian, competition-driven, vacuous non-communities. Sadly,

126

the same applies in a diluted form within middle class culture. These are also forms of alienation as described by Marx, which is not just the preserve of those enduring routine unsatisfactory work – this system doesn't really work for anyone, even those making a huge amount of money.

We dutifully pay our taxes and abide by the law in exchange for being kept safe and being able to access the basics of a civilised life – not a mere dragging, stressful existence where we are (and feel) like expendable commodities rather than people and not to be put on the frontline and on crowded public transport without adequate protection, facing expanded risk and with no one on our side. We do this in the hope that it will be honoured, which is unrealistic because having so much money and power alienates the elite from their humanity. It harms them. It renders them unable to put the protection of human life above the protection of gaining more wealth. Their humanity is disabled by excess and there is no clearer example of this than Trump. But it is important that we remember that he is just one of many like him and those alleged violations are nothing new within those elite spheres. Future Donalds are being prepared faster and in larger quantities than ever before, forever, on a production line of wealth and callous greed, raised on a diet of excess and willing to implement policies, issue Twitter threats, distort reality like it is made out of playdough and simply end press conferences when the questions become too hard to answer. The only solution is to cut the power supply to the production line and what if party politics isn't up for doing that?

There was a social contract of sorts that made this all bearable to the working class and gave a sense of reassurance that things were fairer than they were and a false promise of civility, which should be expected within a G7 country. That contract has long been in shreds and is now tossed casually into the fire. This is where the casually neglected needs of the working class that have for too long found no political voice, force their way to the fore in a way that middle class left politics has failed to do. Simultaneously that long term neglect and mistreatment has since 2010 been gradually encroaching on the middle class like an occupying force which, again, was predicted by Marx. The numbers of those willing to risk their lives, health or livelihoods in protests and outpourings of rage that enough is enough has multiplied as a result. People need to be proper angry to take those risks.

True Costs of a Callous Economic System

Yet the thing about the ingrained complacency of the government and those in positions of influence that fail to challenge them, is that just because things have been the way they are for decades – for many of us our whole lives – that doesn't mean it can't change or change fast, as we have seen in America. They are out of touch. Johnson did not even know what "no recourse to public funds" is, or means, for migrants. I don't think I have yet heard any quizzing of the top team about the Do Not Resuscitate Agreement letters or the lack of palliative care for victims of the virus in care homes at the peak of the crisis.

An extortionate education is no substitute for intelligence or empathy but we can in some ways only hope that their arrogance pushes them ever further toward making more visible mistakes. It may sadly damage and kill people, but social wreckage seems to be what they do, regardless. We need a collective cause so big that the media cannot hide it and threats of armed troops on the streets (or false ridiculous narratives about our party and members) cannot silence it. If we don't act on injustices that affect others, such as being forced back to work too soon, it will unfortunately end up being something more personalised and appalling that finally spurs us into collective action. Corbyn could have been that collective inspiration and almost was, but that hope was successfully stifled and binned. Hopefully it will not take another death to galvanise us to demand better. We should not wait for an emblem of the mass suffering inflicted by the self-alienated at the pinnacle of the unequal power and wealth distribution against those the system holds down at its base and neither should we wait for a celebrity or hero to show us the way.

The widespread and spontaneous response to the death of George Floyd shows us that, for the most part, our human tendency toward kindness and decency remains strongly in place and has hopefully been bolstered by this lockdown episode, where the wealthy nations of the world were able to pause and remember that we are all more dependent on one another than we have been led to believe and that all lives, including black lives, including working class lives, matter and need to be protected and afforded equal respect.

Solidarity with those fighting now for justice and for a saner world. No Justice No Peace.

After the Virus: Building the Post-Capitalist Economy

Howard Thorp @ht4ecosocialism

Amidst the debate about Coronavirus, capitalism, and the future of our economy, the left should be pressing for Green policies. In doing so, we can draw upon ideas set out by Marx and Engels back in the nineteenth century.

It's time we began to think about what kind of economy we're going to have after the Coronavirus. What we can't do is allow the Tory government to introduce a new round of austerity to "pay" for the crisis. And what we must do is ensure that the so-called "low skilled" workers such as shop workers, delivery drivers, bus drivers, care workers, nurses and cleaners who have kept us safe and maintained our economy are properly rewarded for the work they do.

Even in the absence of the virus, in recent times capitalism has shown that it is perfectly capable of bringing about its own demise. This isn't just about the recent collapse of banks, the coming coronavirus "debt crisis" obscures the real problem we face which is the collapse of ecosystems on which we depend for our survival.

Capitalism is not just the driver of the climate crisis we are in, but also of massive environmental degradation, and loss in biodiversity. It is capital accumulation that is devouring our planet and you cannot use the same mechanisms which are destroying the Earth to save it. What we need to do is bring about economic change before the consequences of climate change become unimaginably destructive to our global society. If we are to save the planet, a post-capitalist economy is inevitable, but we can do it the hard way or the better way, and what we need to do is think about how that economy ought to work.

I wonder how many people know that Karl Marx was an admirer of capitalism, in the sense that he admired the huge productive capacity of capitalism, which far exceeded any previous economic system. Marx recognised that if the productive capacity of capitalism was harnessed for the good of society, it could provide people with a much better material standard of living than they ever had before. But he also recognised that, through the mechanism of surplus value, capitalists were able to deprive workers of the wealth that the latter created. There would always be a conflict between capitalists and workers, between the productive forces – workers – and the non-productive forces – capitalists.

Marx understood the massive forces that capitalism could unleash, and Marx and Engels were also much more aware of environmental degradation than they have been given credit for. During the 1870s and 1880s, Engels produced a series of essays applying Marxism to scientific questions. These were posthumously collected in the book *Dialectics of Nature* (published 1925). Engels wrote:

Let us not, however, flatter ourselves overmuch on account of our human victories over nature. For each such victory, nature takes its revenge on us. Each victory, it is true, in the first place brings about the results we expected, but in the second and third places it has quite different, unforeseen, effects which only too often cancel out the first.

As far as climate catastrophe is concerned, the left may have led the way in our understanding of the unfolding climate crisis but the "free" market right have since caught up, and are now pouring their millions into persuading people that climate change is not an issue, through climate change denial, because they are concerned about their profits and the end of domination of democracies by the market. The "free" market fundamentalists are fighting to deny climate change precisely because they recognise that a genuine and meaningful response to climate change will mean the end of capitalism as we know it. This state of affairs was beautifully summed up in an article by Naomi Klein, "Capitalism vs the Climate", in 2011.

So what would a post-capitalist economy look like? It would not mean the end of the private sector, because the private sector is not the same thing as capitalism – your local hairdresser and corner shop owners are not capitalists – but initially it would inevitably mean a much bigger role for the state because a collapsing capitalist economy would have to be replaced by extensive nationalisation of banks, transport and utilities to save them from going under. This is what has already effectively happened with the Coronavirus crisis.

Energy and food production would have to be regulated as would imports and exports. We would need planning in a democratically controlled economy. This would not simply be an ideological choice but a necessary response to crisis. We would have to grow as much of our own food as possible and economies would become much more localised. We would have to rely on walking, cycling and public transport rather than carbon-polluting car use. There have already been plans put forward for a Green New Deal (GND) to reduce carbon emissions and create millions of good green jobs – so we know the way forward. We have the solution in our hands and we must ensure it is implemented.

We are already experiencing problems with climate change in terms of freak weather events, and disruption to agriculture, and we may soon have difficulties with energy supply. During the Coronavirus lockdown we have enjoyed the benefits of cleaner air and exercise, and this needs to continue into the future. We have a choice, we can begin to adjust our economy now, to deal with these problems, or we can carry on with "business as usual" and inevitably face much worse conditions later. We already have the basis of a GND in Labour's policy programme. We need to make sure that this remains at the top of our agenda and is the ground on which we fight the next General Election. We must work together to create a new kind of economy to deal with possibly the greatest challenge that human beings have ever faced.

Take it on the Chin: Conservatism and COVID

@AndrewGodsell

The callous nature of the Conservatives, with their disregard for vulnerable people plus our NHS, have been sharply exposed by the COVID crisis. A Blog post from May 2020.

The Coronavirus COVID-19 pandemic has tragically killed over 280,000 people throughout the world. Officially 31,855 people in the United Kingdom have died as a result of COVID, at the time of my writing this, May 10 2020. Today Boris Johnson has announced plans to ease the lockdown (to the horror of many people). Our nation is experiencing an unusually high percentage death rate among confirmed cases, compared to the world average. There is public expectation of a major inquiry into the mistakes made, including many by the Conservative government, in dealing with COVID.

The mainstream media view is that Johnson, himself recently hospitalised by the disease, and the government he leads on an intermittent basis, are competently fighting a valiant battle to save the nation from the disease. The failings of the government have, however, been so severe that even political reporters and newscasters at the BBC – the supposedly public broadcaster which gave Johnson such an easy ride during the last General Election – have been expressing some reservations.

Outside the MSM bubble, large sections of the population, including many NHS staff and other key workers, have displayed trenchant criticism of a muddled government response. For far too long, the Conservatives placed their support of the capitalist economy, and big business – the natural plus financial friends of the Tories – ahead of the need to save lives, and protect the wider community.

An official inquiry could be months, or years, away. Any completion of such a process, and implementation of recommendations, will follow even later – as we have seen in numerous cases of state failure, ranging from the Hillsborough disaster to the Grenfell Tower fire. Before scrutiny of any of the important issues debated during the early stage of the COVID outbreak possibly fades, a look back to the initial government response may help as a reminder. The rot had set in even before COVID reached Britain.

On January 23 2020, Matt Hancock, Secretary of State for Health, made the first government statement to Parliament about the implications of the outbreak of a new form of Coronavirus, at Wuhan, in China, during the final weeks of 2019. Hancock said:

We have been closely monitoring the situation in Wuhan and have put in place proportionate precautionary measures. Our approach has at all times been guided by the advice of the Chief Medical Officer, Professor Chris Whitty....The Chief Medical Officer has revised the risk to the UK population from "very low" to "low", and has concluded that, while there is an increased likelihood that cases may arise in this country, we are well-prepared and well-equipped to deal with them. The UK is one of the first countries to have developed a world-leading test for the new Coronavirus. The NHS is ready to respond appropriately to any cases that emerge. Clinicians in both primary and secondary care have already received advice, covering initial detection and investigation of possible cases, infection prevention and control, and clinical diagnostics....The public can be assured that the whole of the UK is always well-prepared for these types of outbreaks, and we will remain vigilant and keep our response under constant review in the light of emerging scientific evidence.

The statement aimed to offer assurance but, within weeks, it became clear that Tory ministers were alarmingly complacent. The message from Hancock was shown to be dangerously wrong in several respects.

The first COVID cases in the UK were diagnosed on January 31, just eight days after Hancock and Whitty thought the risk to be "low". The risk level had been moved to "moderate" on January 30, but the government took little action to alert the public to the scale of the danger during February.

Johnson announced, on March 3, "I was at a hospital the other night, where I think a few there were actually Coronavirus patients, and I shook hands with everybody, you'll be pleased to know, and I continue to shake hands". Johnson's handshakes were politeness turned into pure irresponsibility.

The first death occurred on March 5, and Johnson belatedly attended the Cabinet's emergency COBRA committee on March 9, after he had missed the five preceding meetings on the subject of

133

Coronavirus. The risk level for the UK was not escalated from "moderate" to "high" until March 12.

The government, and its scientific advisors, favoured the idea of attempting to create "Herd Immunity", with Johnson saying in a national television interview "one of the theories is that perhaps you could take it on the chin, take it all in one go and allow the disease, as it were, to move through the population, without taking as many draconian measures". Laymen pointed out the massive number of deaths that would be likely in Britain, before the remainder of the population could hope for "Herd Immunity". The government and their scientists backed down, but the strategy remained far from clear.

The Cheltenham Festival horse race meeting went ahead as usual – allegedly due to gambling companies lobbying the government against possible cancellation – with crowds of around 60,000 people per day, something that was soon shown to have spread COVID. Other sports events were postponed, upon the decision of various organising bodies, rather than government direction. For several weeks, the response of Johnson and his government was complacent, until pressure from NHS staff, a Labour Party wisely led (at that point) by Jeremy Corbyn, and the wider public, prompted action, as the death toll rose. Daily life continued much as usual, until the government belatedly started to recommend social distancing, and closed schools. Johnson did not announce the much-delayed effective lockdown until March 23.

Rishi Sunak, the new Tory Chancellor of the Exchequer, following the departure of Sajid Javid – who clashed with Dominic Cummings, the power behind the Johnson throne – delivered a multi-billion pound emergency financial package. The Tories celebrated Sunak's role, but other people asked why the "Magic Money Tree", which Theresa May said in 2017 did not exist, and therefore could not produce a pay rise for nurses, had suddenly sprouted the green shoots of a massive capitalist bailout. It was similar to the taxpayer rescue of the banks during the 2008-09 financial crisis – a time when Javid and Sunak were speculative bankers.

Returning to the claims of Matt Hancock, there has been little evidence of the UK being a world leader in testing for COVID. Johnson and Hancock have announced various targets to test 10,000 people per day, then 25,000, followed by 100,000, and the latest aim is 200,000, but progress has generally fallen short of intention. Despite great public campaigning to get patients, NHS clinical staff, carers, more key workers, and masses of vulnerable people, rapidly tested, for many weeks it was clear that this was not happening at a sufficient scale. The government also failed to ensure that the private sector could produce, and deliver, sufficient testing capacity.

Hancock declared the NHS to be ready for the spread of the illness, back in January. In the following months, testimony from NHS staff and patients showed this had not been true, and was still not true. Already hard-pressed hospitals suddenly had to deal with additional admissions of COVID patients. There was a shortage of ventilators, despite claims by the government that they were urgently arranging to increase production and acquisition, and many frontline health workers lacked the required Personal Protective Equipment.

TORY VOTERS.
AT THE NEXT ELECTION,

NHS

STAY HOME,
PROTECT THE NHS,
SAVE LIVES.

As events unfolded, it was clear that Hancock, Johnson, and their friends in government, were not vigilant. They were slow to take action, and much of that action was indecisive – until the government were reluctantly forced to fall in line with the plans advocated by other people.

This complacent attitude has led to the official total of over 31,000 deaths. It is sadly clear that thousands more people have died due to COVID, but are excluded from that total, as they were not tested for the disease. A study published by the *Financial Times* – traditionally a Tory-supporting newspaper – estimated the real UK death toll to be 41,000 on April 21. At that time, the official figure was 17,000 deaths. Hancock and Whitty should be sacked for their fatal mistakes, but they continue to shape policy, and defend it with evasive comments at daily press conferences.

Many Conservative MPs have publicly called for the lockdown to be rapidly lifted, with their priority being the strength of the economy (code for the income of party funders). The Tories tell us that capitalism is the world's greatest economic system, with centuries of proven success. Why do they think that a few weeks of COVID lockdown could destroy their beloved capitalism? Could the real answer be Socialism and a planned economy?

The tragic failings of the Tories over COVID are sadly predictable, repeating the pattern of a cruel decade of austerity, in which the rich minority have got richer, while millions of people have struggled. In 2017, an academic study, projecting figures from the increase in the death rate since the Conservatives took power in 2010, suggested that 120,000 people had died prematurely as a result of austerity. Consistent under-funding, and privatisation, of the NHS have been a major feature of austerity, and this in turn has contributed to tens of thousands of preventable deaths in the COVID crisis.

A Deep Burning Hatred for the Tory Party

@Rachael_Swindon

A Twitter thread from May 2020.

I have spent years disliking the Conservatives, and what they stand for. That's no secret. The last decade has been a miserable time for millions of people, me included. That's no secret. But they've got my disliking and turned it in to a deep and burning hatred.

Every single day we see the Covid death toll climb, and our hearts shatter for the bereaved families.

What makes this worse is one indisputable fact: the government's catastrophically inept response to the arrival of Covid-19 has cost lives.

Now let's be certain of something else. Conservative austerity cost hundreds of thousands of lives. There was no daily death toll for the British people that died as a result of austerity. Boris Johnson refuses to use the word "austerity". He knows what they did to us.

I'll fight for the victims of austerity until my final breath. Now the thing is, austerity was mainly targeted at the poorest and most vulnerable in society. To be clear, the governments of Cameron, May and Johnson are criminals.

This fight won't end soon. The big difference with Covid, it doesn't discriminate between rich and poor. The poor and vulnerable, as well as BAME people, are taking the brunt of this hideous virus, but it is attacking everyone, in a way austerity never did.

While they downgraded your A&E, and closed down your Sure Start Centres, they were handing out more than £90 billion in corporate welfare, in one year alone.

These were political choices. None of it happened by accident. So that gives you an idea of what I think about the Tories.

But here's the thing. I *desperately* wanted them to succeed with the Coronavirus crisis. Surely that's normal? But they haven't succeeded. Let's not pretend otherwise.

I can't actually put the hatred in to words to be honest. The handling of the crisis has been like witnessing a slow motion motorway pile-up. When the world went into lockdown, Boris Johnson went on holiday. Just think about that for a moment. The pathetic effort of a lockdown was already too late.

Hundreds of healthcare heroes have died. They sent them to fight an invisible enemy dressed in bin bags and eBay face masks. We sent our own minimal stocks of PPE to China? Why?

A doctor sent a Tweet to Johnson, warning him of the consequences of the PPE crisis. He died 2 weeks later. Matt Hancock had a chance to apologise to the doctor's grieving son, on live radio, but he refused. Hancock wanted everyone to know what a great job he had done of keeping the pressure off the NHS. In reality, hospitals sent elderly patients with Covid-19 in to care homes, with little or no palliative care.

This is a national scandal. We've had the testing debacle, a virtually anonymous Prime Minister, and a Cabinet that would be out of their depth in a single drop of rain. We've had the plane loads of faulty PPE from Turkey, and an unelected bureaucrat briefing the media with stories of lockdown freedom. We've had them using international comparisons until the comparisons began to reveal the scale of the unfolding tragedy.

We've had herd immunity spoken about, because they "follow the science" apparently. We've had Johnson and his "take it on the chin" comments. We've had a randy scientist, and bullying Cabinet Ministers thrown at us to distract from their failures. We've had the awful spectacle of Johnson clapping NHS heroes, while giving them a real terms wage cut by way of thanks. Hideous hypocrite.

We've had few media voices to ask the difficult questions. Piers Morgan and James O'Brien are hardly idols of mine, but they've absolutely smashed it. Genuinely.

We've had a 100 year old hero dragging himself up and down his garden to raise millions for an underfunded NHS.

We've had them tell us less than 20,000 deaths would be a "good result". The current death toll could actually be treble that number. We've had Boris Johnson claim "success", cheered on by his complicit Cabinet and the billionaire-owned media.

At a time when Britain needed calm, efficient and strong leadership, we ended up with Boris Johnson, Gove, Patel, Raab, Jenrick and Dominic Cummings.

I'm afraid Tory voters need to own their vote, and take a look at what they've done. The anger will not subside. The injustices won't just disappear. We will keep fighting.

This isn't a left / right issue, it's a right / wrong issue. It's a crisis that demands ownership, and that squarely falls at the door of Number 10 Downing Street.

Honestly, the government are fucking monsters. Every death is collateral damage for them. The platitudes make me want to violently vomit. Each and every one of them disgust me. I absolutely despise this hideous abomination of a government.

Suggestions for Further Reading

Books

Salvador Allende *Chile's Road to Socialism* (1973)

Tony Benn *Arguments for Socialism* (1980)

Tony Benn *Arguments for Democracy* (1981)

Tony Benn *The Future for Socialism (Agenda for the Twenty-first Century)* (1991)

Tony Benn *The Benn Diaries: Single Volume Edition 1940–90* (1995)

Tony Benn *The Best of Benn* (Edited by Ruth Winstone, 2014)

Aneurin Bevan *Why Not Trust the Tories?* (1944)

Aneurin Bevan *In Place of Fear* (1952)

H N Brailsford *The War of Steel and Gold: A Study of the Armed Peace* (1914)

Beatrix Campbell *The Iron Ladies: Why Do Women Vote Tory?* (1987)

Cassius (Michael Foot) *The Trial of Mussolini* (1943)

Cato (Michael Foot, Frank Owen, and Peter Howard) *Guilty Men* (1940)

Noam Chomsky *Occupy* (2012)

Noam Chomsky and Ilan Pappe *On Palestine* (2015)

Maurice Cornforth (Editor) *Rebels and Their Causes: Essays in Honour of A L Morton* (1978)

Regis Debray *Conversations with Allende: Socialism in Chile* (1971)

Maurice Dobb *Studies in the Development of Capitalism* (1946)

Friedrich Engels *The Condition of the Working Class in England* (1845)

Friedrich Engels *Dialectics of Nature* (1925)

Giuseppe Fiori *Antonio Gramsci: Life of a Revolutionary* (1970)

Mark Fisher *Capitalist Realism: Is There No Alternative?* (2009)

Michael Foot and Donald Bruce *Who Are the Patriots?* (1949)

Michael Foot *Aneurin Bevan: 1897-1945* (1962)
Aneurin Bevan: 1945-1960 (1973)

Michael Foot *Debts of Honour* (1980)

Michael Foot *Another Heart and Other Pulses: The Alternative to the Thatcher Society* (1984)

Michael Foot *Loyalists and Loners* (1986)

William Gallacher *Revolt on the Clyde* (1936)

Andrew Gamble *The Conservative Nation* (1974)

George Gissing *Workers in the Dawn* (1880)

Andrew Godsell *Why NOT Trust the CONservatives?* (2015)

Antonio Gramsci *Selections From Prison Notebooks* (Edited by Quinton Hoare and Geoffrey Nowell Smith, 1971)

Stuart Hall and Martin Jacques (Editors) *The Politics of Thatcherism* (1983)

Stuart Hall *The Hard Road to Renewal: Thatcherism and the Crisis of the Left* (1988)

Christopher Hampton (Editor) *A Radical Reader: The Struggle For Change in England, 1381-1914* (1984)

Michael Hardt and Antonio Negri *Empire* (2000)

Michael Hardt and Antonio Negri *Multitude: War and Democracy in the Age of Empire* (2004)

Michael Hardt and Antonio Negri *Commonwealth* (2009)

Eric Heffer *Labour's Future – Socialist or SDP Mark 2?* (1986)

Eric Hobsbawm *Labouring Men: Studies in the History of Labour* (1964)

Eric Hobsbawm *Industry and Empire: From 1750 to the Present Day* (1968)

Eric Hobsbawm *How to Change the World: Tales of Marx and Marxism* (2011)

Ted Honderich *Conservatism: Burke, Nozick, Bush, Blair?* (2005)

Mark Jenkins *Bevanism: Labour's High Tide – The Cold War and the Democratic Mass Movement* (1979)

Gerald Kaufman (Editor) *Renewal: Labour's Britain in the 1980s* (1983)

Peter Kropotkin *The Conquest of Bread* (1892)

Peter Kropotkin *Fields, Factories, and Workshops* (1899)

Vladimir Lenin *Imperialism: The Highest Stage of Capitalism* (1917)

Vladimir Lenin *The State and Revolution* (1917)

Rosa Luxembourg *The Accumulation of Capital: A Contribution to an Economic Explanation of Imperialism* (1913)

Karl Marx and Friedrich Engels *The Communist Manifesto* (1848)

Karl Marx *Capital: A Critique of Political Economy*
Volume 1 (1867)
Volume 2 (Edited by Friedrich Engels, 1885)
Volume 3 (Edited by Friedrich Engels, 1894)

Karl Marx and Friedrich Engels *Articles on Britain* (1971)

Mariana Mazzucato *The Value of Everything: Making and Taking in the Global Economy* (2018)

Ralph Miliband *The State in Capitalist Society* (1969)

William Morris *A Dream of John Ball* (1888)

William Morris *News From Nowhere* (1890)

William Morris *The Political Writings of William Morris* (Edited by A L Morton, 1984)

A L Morton *A People's History of England* (1938)

A L Morton *The English Utopia* (1952)

Alex Nunns *The Candidate: Jeremy Corbyn's Improbable Path to Power* (2016)

George Orwell *The Road to Wigan Pier* (1937)

George Orwell *Homage to Catalonia* (1938)

George Orwell *The Lion and the Unicorn: Socialism and the English Genius* (1941)

George Orwell *Animal Farm* (1945)

George Orwell *Nineteen Eighty-Four* (1949)

Thomas Paine *Common Sense* (1776)

Thomas Paine *Rights of Man* (1791)

Pierre-Joseph Proudhon *What is Property?* (1840)

Alistair J Reid and Henry Pelling *A Short History of the Labour Party* (2005)

John Ross *Thatcher and Friends: The Anatomy of the Tory Party* (1983)

George Bernard Shaw (Editor) *Fabian Essays in Socialism* (1889)

Joss Sheldon *Individutopia* (2018)

Dennis Skinner *Sailing Close to the Wind: Reminiscences* (2014)

John Strachey *Why You Should be a Socialist* (1938)

John Strachey *The Strangled Cry and Other Unparliamentary Papers* (1962)

R H Tawney *The Acquisitive Society* (1920)

R H Tawney *Equality* (1931)

R H Tawney *The Attack and Other Papers* (1953 – reprinted in 1981 with a Foreword by Tony Benn)

R H Tawney *The Radical Tradition: Twelve Essays on Politics, Education, and Literature* (Edited by Rita Hinden, 1964)

E P Thompson *The Making of the English Working Class* (1963)

Robert Tressell *The Ragged-Trousered Philanthropists* (1914)

Leon Trotsky *The Basic Writings of Trotsky* (Edited by Irving Howe, 1964)

Yanis Varoufakis *And the Weak Suffer What They Must?: Europe, Austerity and the Threat to Global Stability* (2016)

Sidney and Beatrice Webb *A Constitution for the Socialist Commonwealth of Great Britain* (1920)

H G Wells *New Worlds For Old* (1908)

H G Wells *The Shape of Things to Come* (1933)

Emile Zola *Germinal* (1885)

Independent Media Websites and Radical Blogs

All That is Solid

Another Angry Voice

Byline Times

The Canary

Dorset Eye

Double Down News

The Equality Trust

Evolve Politics

Labour Heartlands

Left Foot Forward

Media Diversified

Media Lens

Morning Star

Mutual Interest

Novara Media

Open Democracy

The Pileus

The Poor Side of Life

The Prole Star

Ramblings of an Ordinary Man

The Skwawkbox

Socialist Action

True Publica

UK Column

Unity News

Vox Political

Why NOT Trust the CONservatives?

Andrew Godsell

A critical history of the Conservative Party, from its formation in 1830 through to the premiership of David Cameron. The record of the Conservatives in government and Parliament is surveyed, along with the organisation and outlook of the party.

Throwing original light on British politics, this radical interpretation of its subject offers telling observations on many notorious Tories, including Robert Peel, Benjamin Disraeli, Lord Salisbury, Andrew Bonar Law, Stanley Baldwin, Neville Chamberlain, Harold Macmillan, Edward Heath, Margaret Thatcher, and John Major.

The original version of this book was the first critical history of the Conservatives ever published, filling a notable omission in British political literature, and remained in print for a quarter of a century. The work received approving comments from Neil Kinnock, Ken Livingstone, Larry Whitty, and Ted Honderich. This reissue extends the terrible tale of the Tories into the twenty first century.

Printed in Great Britain
by Amazon